# HOME SEWING

*Couture*
# TECHNIQUES

First published in the UK in 2009 by
Apple Press
7 Greenland Street
London NW1 0ND
United Kingdom
www.apple-press.com

ISBN 978-1-84543-307-9

10 9 8 7 6 5 4 3 2 1

Technical Editor: Carol Spier
Copy Editor: Karen Levy
Proofreader: Jennifer Bright Reich
Book & Cover Design: Kathie Alexander
Page Layout: Kathie Alexander
Photographs: Images on pages 7, 11, 16, 35, 44, 47, 116, 120,
129, 131, 162, 173, 174 by Jack Deutsch Photography, Images
on pages 9, 13, and 14 (top) by Glenn Scott Photography

Printed in Singapore

# HOME SEWING

## Couture
# TECHNIQUES

### Creating Designer-Quality Fashion

*Kenneth D. King*

**APPLE**

# *Contents*

# INTRODUCTION

# MY BAG OF *Tricks*

Some of my customers ask me, "Why are you writing a book?" It is simply because writing gives me a chance to talk to an audience that speaks the same language of sewing—an audience that, like me, considers sewing a passion. Besides, nobody at the parties I go to understands my sewing jokes!

For those of you who don't know much about me, I started sewing when I was young and worked in window display before becoming a designer. Display was useful training, because a good display person has to have a working knowledge of a broad range of subjects. This training taught me to bring together information from different disciplines to achieve a desired result.

I have little formal sewing training beyond pattern drafting, which I learned from a French-trained teacher. All my sewing skills are self-taught. In certain respects, this was beneficial, because I was just ignorant enough of the facts to do what I wanted. This lack of formal training led me to find some rather unorthodox solutions to construction problems.

I am one of the fortunate few who is able to make a livelihood from a vocation that is also a passion. Because I am deeply interested in what I do—and because I sell to a very demanding market—I need to create superbly finished and well-performing products that also generate a profit. This fact is most important, and I have learned to conceive techniques that will give me the proper finish while also making good use of my time.

There are techniques in this book that are shown in my first book, but there are new ways that I've learned to approach many of them since it was published, so I've updated them here. Also included are some new tricks and techniques that I've discovered in the past several years. It's a pleasure to revisit the past and also to share with all of my readers the experience I've gained since the first book came out. These techniques have many applications for everyone who sews. With a little practice and some creative thinking, you will be able to make some pieces that will amaze you!

In the sewing literature available today, there is an emphasis on shortcuts and other time-saving procedures. Some of them are useful, but some produce results that look like you were trying to save time or money! I believe it's better to spend a bit more time with a project and achieve something very special, rather than try to save time or money by sewing running shorts and T-shirts. Let the factories that can do that kind of work more cost-effectively make those things. Extra time in today's hectic world is indeed a luxury. When taking time for sewing, make that luxury count!

This book is not project-oriented. It's devoted to techniques. One reason for this is that I regard techniques as tools, or what I refer to as my "bag of tricks." All the information on each subject is arranged in a separate section. So, if your interest is sewing with velvet, for example, you'll find all my tricks for working with velvet in one place. Although I hope you will just sit down and read through the book, from cover to cover, I know this expectation is not realistic. A very wise woman once told me that it's not necessary to carry all you need to know in your head, you only have to know

where to get your hands on the information when you need it. Familiarise yourself with the book, and then refer to it when you need it.

You will also notice that I often refer to the "piece" in the text rather than to the "garment." These techniques need not be restricted to apparel sewing. You can also apply them to home decor and craft sewing. The same logic and concepts apply, whether you're sewing clothing, home furnishings, or crafts. My hope is that this book will make traveling across the sewing spectrum a more rewarding journey for you.

My wish is for this book to stimulate your sense of creativity and adventure. Don't be afraid to experiment with my techniques. By getting creative, you can invent your own ways of doing things. In sewing there are no absolutes.

I hope to meet you, as I teach and travel, and hear how these techniques directed you to find your own creative solutions to new sewing challenges. Until then, enjoy this book!

# CHAPTER 1

# *Choosing* FABRICS

The choice of fashion fabric is an entirely personal decision. If a fabric speaks to you, ignore family and friends, and even your own better judgment, and just use it. Here are some words of wisdom on some difficult fabrics.

The fabrics that are most apt to cause problems are velvet, moiré, faille (also known as bengaline), ottoman, and satin. Once you know the pitfalls of working with these fabrics, you will feel more comfortable dealing with them.

→ Velvet, especially crushed velvet, is one of the most luxurious fabrics. Its drape and surface texture are shown to advantage in this velvet evening wrap.

# $\mathcal{V}$elvet

Velvet is one of those fabrics that is often referred to as having psychological components. One component is the expectation of weight. Another is the expectation of thickness or a "cushion." When you put your hands on velvet, you expect your fingers to just sink into it.

To achieve these effects when working with velvet, interline all pieces with cotton flannel (see page 15). Interlining with cotton flannel gives the fabric a richer hand, or feel. It also makes the velvet hang more beautifully. Interlining also allows you to hand-tack the seam allowances with a catch stitch, page 10 (I often call this a featherstitch, but it isn't the stitch embroiderers know by that name), eliminating any topstitching that might be needed to control seam allowances. The very idea of topstitching velvet gives some folks nightmares!

After preshrinking the interlining, cut the project pieces first out of the flannel and then out of the velvet. Mark all your seamlines on the flannel piece. Treat the two pieces as one by tailor-basting them together with silk thread, as shown in the drawing above right. The silk thread will prevent needle and thread marks from showing on the velvet.

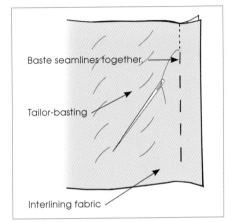

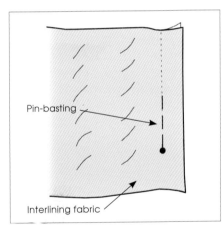

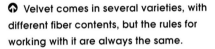

Velvet comes in several varieties, with different fiber contents, but the rules for working with it are always the same.

When sewing velvet to a flat-surfaced fabric, there is no way around it—baste as if your life depended on it! Once the seamlines are marked on the flannel interlining, the "creep" in velvet can be controlled by hand- or pin-basting the two pieces to be joined along the seamline for more accurate sewing. For velvet-to-velvet seams, pin-basting can be substituted.

Stitch quality is most important when sewing on velvet, especially when sewing straight seams, which have a tendency to pucker. Because you are working with some thickness, choose a stitch length that is longer than normal. A slight zig-zag also helps minimize the puckering. A walking foot is an absolute necessity for controlling all of the layers. Buy one— you will bless the day you did.

## SEWING MACHINE SETTINGS FOR VELVET

*Stitch:* Zigzag
*Stitch Width:* 0.5 mm
*Stitch Length:* 3.0–3.5 mm

⬆ **Mohair velvet, which is an upholstery fabric, is the absolute best surface for pressing velvets and other napped fabrics.**

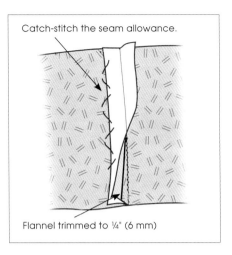

Catch-stitch the seam allowance.

Flannel trimmed to ¼" (6 mm)

After you have sewn the seams comes the arduous task of pressing. Most stitchers prefer to press velvet by placing it face down on either a heavy towel or a velvet pressing board. Many people end up crushing the nap of the fabric at the edge of the board, however, because most velvet pressing boards are on the small side.

From my design experience, I have found that the best surface for pressing velvet is mohair velvet. Remember that prickly velvet sofa your grandmother had? That fabric is mohair velvet, which is still made today for upholstery.

Purchase a piece that is large enough to cover the entire surface of your pressing table. A large pressing surface is particularly helpful when pressing pieces with long seams, such as a full-length skirt. There is no edge on which to mar the nap, and there is no need to move the pressing board as you press the long seam. When you compare them by size, a piece of mohair velvet is far less expensive than a velvet board.

Before pressing your work, trim the seam allowances of the flannel to ¼" (6 mm). To press, lay the piece flat, right side down, on the mohair velvet. Steam- and finger-press the seams open. (If you are working with an industrial steam iron, keep the iron well away from the fabric, because the heavy jets of steam will crush the nap.) Test the steam on an extra piece of fabric first.

**ZIGZAG STITCH** *tip*

The zigzag stitch is especially effective on velvet fabric when the seam falls on the bias, as in a gored skirt. The stitch is long enough to minimize the puckering, and the zigzag builds in additional stretch.

After you have pressed the seams, attach the seam allowances to the flannel with a catch stitch, as shown in the drawing on the facing page. Along with thickness, weight is another expectation of velvet. The flannel interlining does add some weight, but you can add additional weight by interfacing the hem with bias strips of wool melton, making a soft fold at the hem.

Or interface the hem with horsehair braid and add weights along the hem. This technique works especially well with gored skirts or swing-back coats. Attach the weights where the seamlines meet the hem. The weighted interfacing controls the drape quite nicely and allows for graceful movement when the piece is in motion. Be careful, though—too much weight can make the piece feel oppressive when worn.

To cover the weights, cut a piece of fabric or felt twice the diameter of the weight plus ¹⁄₂" (1.3 cm) all around for seam allowances. Fold the fabric in half, as shown in the drawing at right. Working with an adjustable zipper foot, stitch the weight into the fold of the fabric, running the foot along the edge of the weight. Grade the seam allowances and hand-stitch the covered weight into the piece. One tip: To keep the edges of the weight from showing up during pressing, hammer them flat with a regular hammer before you cover them.

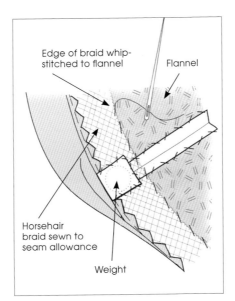

Edge of braid whip-stitched to flannel

Flannel

Horsehair braid sewn to seam allowance

Weight

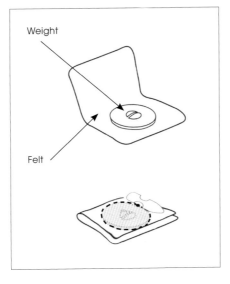

Weight

Felt

*tip*

**PADDING**

When making velvet collars and cuffs, pad the interlined velvet with a thin layer of cotton or wool batting (don't use polyester, whatever anyone says, as it may "bleed" through the velvet). This extra padding technique is also effective for hats, handbags, or any other items for which you want to create a feeling of luxury.

⊙ **Ruched black velvet contrasts with transparent black organza in this high-collared evening coat.**

# Faille, Moiré, and Ottoman

Faille (or bengaline), moiré, and ottoman are often referred to as "corded" fabrics. The warp (lengthwise) threads are finer than the heavy cotton weft (crosswise) threads. In faille and moiré, the fine weft threads are packed closely together, but in ottoman the heavier weft cords are spaced further apart. This method of construction creates a ribbed effect along the crosswise grain.

These fabrics may shrink under steam. The degree of shrinkage depends on the thickness of the crosswise threads and whether or not there was pressure used in the finishing process. In the moiré finishing process, the optical effect of the moiré pattern is heat-pressed onto the ribbed surface of the fabric. Therefore, with moirés, avoid preshrinking like the plague! Because the crosswise threads are cotton (a natural fiber), the moiré effect will not last under steam—the fibers will plump up, and the moiré effect will be diminished or lost. It's okay to preshrink with steam before cutting into ottomans and failles.

When pressing these three types of fabrics, also be careful not to create impressions of the fabric against itself. Work with a pressing surface covered with cotton drill cloth or any other smooth covering to avoid creating undesired textures on the fabrics.

These fabrics are suitable for vests and tailored clothing (and for home furnishings). Because they are somewhat perishable—meaning they're prone to abrasion and will split under stress—be sure to always add an interlining of some sort. Also, because they are thin, they will look "hammered" unless fabric is underneath to support them. For clothing, siri cotton or cotton flannel work quite nicely. In home furnishings, cotton flannel or wool flannel produce good results.

 The sheen and ribbed surface of these fabrics provide drama and texture to evening clothes.

*tip* **SCOTCHGARD SPRAY**
When sewing a white or extremely light-colored rayon moiré or faille, Scotchgard the fabric to death to help keep it fresh. But test first on a scrap; Scotchgard is water-based and could leave a mark on these fabrics.

# $\mathcal{S}$atin

Satin makes great linings and gives a piece nice body. There are different types of satin, such as slipper satin (also known as bridal satin), duchesse satin (which has a slightly more matte finish), and crepe-backed satin (also known as satin-backed crepe, go figure). These kinds of satin can come in different weights, and whenever possible, go for a heavier weight. The thinner ones will look cheap when made up. These types can be either man-made or natural fibers, which may or may not affect the cost. Fiber content is important here only in that you need to know what temperature to set your iron to. I myself like the man-made fibers just as well as the natural ones, and I prefer them in situations where the piece will receive heavy wear. For most purposes—whether apparel or home furnishings—work with a heavy slipper satin.

When marking satin, work with a marking wheel that has either a smooth edge or blunted points. Sharp, pointed wheels will tear the fabric. When making tailor's tacks on satin, use silk thread and a number 10 beading needle. Use the beading needle and silk thread for any thread tracing or basting you need, too.

When working with satin for tailored garments or outer garments (or for home furnishing), you need to interline it. Interline apparel with cotton flannel. Interline home projects with cotton or a cotton/polyester blend twill, which will take the strain of daily use.

Press satin with a dry iron. Steam just makes the surface of satin "wobbly" and is best only for a soft press—for example, on the luxurious lining of an evening wrap. After pressing the seam as sewn, soft press by laying the seam wrong side up over the seam roll and steaming lightly to create a cushioned effect, finger-pressing the seam allowances open to form a softly creased seamline.

To hard-press a satin seam open, first press the seam as sewn, then press it open on a hard wooden seam roll that is covered with cotton drill cloth (see "Pressing Tools," page 20).

⬆ Satin is a popular fabric for both eveningwear and bridal attire. Its lustrous surface is attractive, but any imperfections in your sewing will show. Follow my tips to give your satin projects a polished look.

# Understructure Fabrics

Remember this: The fashion fabric is only along for the ride! The understructure materials are essential. Some of the materials referred to in this book are unorthodox and are often not used as the manufacturer intended. All interfacings referred to are sew-in interfacings, unless otherwise noted. Unless indicated, preshrinking is necessary for all understructures. The preferred method is to take wool fabrics to a dry cleaner and have them heavily steamed. You can wash and dry cotton fabrics at home.

## Wool

Wool felt adds heft and thickness to a piece and should contain as high a percentage of wool as possible. Use wool felt to interline small pieces, to spot-interline large ones, and to interface hems for a better drape.

If wool felt is not available, use wool flannel. Wool flannel is warm, so it's a good choice as interlining for evening wraps or coats. If the piece only needs nice heft or weight, choose cotton flannel instead. If you wash wool flannel in hot water and dry it at a high temperature, you will create your own wool felt.

Wool melton is a coat fabric that is very useful for thickening collars and interfacing the hems of jackets. It's also a good substitute for wool felt (although a relatively expensive one). If you are creating a flat tailored sleeve head, wool melton is a good choice. Buy end-of-bolt pieces from the remnant tables. Buying it from the regular-priced bolt can be expensive.

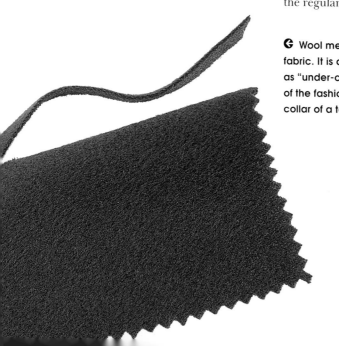

↻ Wool melton is a dense, thick coat fabric. It is also sold at tailors' suppliers as "under-collar cloth" and used instead of the fashion fabric for making the under collar of a tailored jacket.

## Canvas

Hair canvas is a good fabric to use as interfacing for tailored clothes. Hymo brand is the best choice (canvas sometimes is referred to as "hymo" as a generic term, such as we refer to "Kleenex" as something to wipe our noses with) because of its drape and weight. It's made from a blend of wool and goat hair, which causes the Hymo to "stick" to the fashion fabric. Avoid fusible hair canvas when working with the techniques presented in this book.

## Horsehair canvas

Horsehair canvas or haircloth is available in two varieties. Although it's traditionally made from real horsehair, another type is made from nylon. Real horsehair is the way to go if you can find it. It's 18" to 20" wide (45.5 to 51 cm)—the length of the horse's tail—with the hair strands running in the crosswise grain. Nylon horsehair is sometimes wider.

The characteristics that make this fabric so useful in construction are the stability on the crosswise grain and the relative fluidity of the lengthwise grain. In jackets, use horsehair canvas for shields and flat shoulder pads (see pages 112 and 117). You can also use haircloth for cut-and-sewn hats. Stiffening with haircloth is better for this type of hat because the material springs back into shape when crushed. Buckram, another type of millinery stiffener, eventually loses its starch.

↑ Horsehair canvas is also known as haircloth. It is the support behind the support for hair canvas.

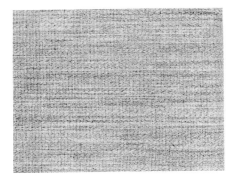

↑ When tailoring a jacket or coat, you need support underneath to achieve a crisp silhouette. Hair canvas (also known as canvas) will do the job.

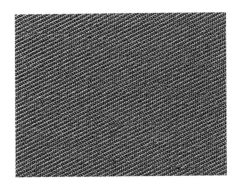

↑ Twill fabric for underlining is best known as denim, which proved its strength in the Wild West.

## Twill

Twill fabric is the best type of interlining for pieces that will receive stress through stretch, such as home decorating projects. For the things I do, I use a jeans-weight twill fabric. It is strong, gives the piece body, and is relatively inexpensive. You can use natural fiber, polyester, or a blend here. Fiber content isn't the issue—the inherent structure of the fabric is. As for preshrinking, you don't do it when the piece will be dry-cleaned and needs not to stretch, such as a bustier, which depends on staying at a fixed circumference and not stretching to be successful. You can preshrink for home décor items that will be washed or dry-cleaned. Run the lengthwise grainline parallel to the line of stretch to absorb the stress on the fashion fabric.

## Cotton flannel

Cotton flannel (also called flannelette) is a favorite for interlinings. The type of flannel common in babies' nightwear and children's pajamas makes good interlining. It is inexpensive (especially in end-of-bolt pieces on the discount tables). It also provides a little comic relief to know that inside a couture piece lies a teddy bear print. Drapery interlining flannel, also known as bump cloth, is quite sumptuous and hangs well; you might like to try it for garments. Cotton flannel works well with silks, lightweight jacquards, moirés, and failles.

↑ Cotton flannel is one of my secret weapons for tailoring thinner fabrics such as fine jacquards.

## Siri

Siri is a shirt-weight, plain-weave cotton that gives body without as much weight as cotton flannel does. It is known also as cotton broadcloth and shirting cotton. It can be found in the section of the fabric store that sells the blouse-weight fabrics. Siri is appropriate for interlining slightly heavier fabrics, such as moiré or faille, where the hem stitches or the tacking stitches on facings would show through.

Armo Press Soft is used interchangeably with siri cotton. This product is often pulled off-grain when it is wound onto the bolt, so check the grainline and straighten it before cutting.

## Cotton batiste

Cotton batiste works nicely under wool crepe, when you need a slight bit of control to help the garment keep its shape. Batiste also works well for making the half-back interfacing pieces for tailored jackets (see page 111).

## Organza

Organza can be either polyester or silk. Polyester has more bounce, but it may or may not be to your taste when pressing. (If used to underline an entire bodice, it also makes the garment too warm to wear.) Organza works well as interlining or facing for bias-cut bodices or other slinky dresses, where lightweight interlining and a slight bit of control at the bust are desired. It also makes terrific stay tape and is good for interfacing pocket welts without creating bulk.

## Heavy net

Heavy net (sometimes called cape net) is great for stiffening laces, creating petticoats, and making supports for those "man-eating" puffed sleeves. To give you an idea of how stiff this net is, compare nylon net to silk tulle. Heavy net is to nylon net what nylon net is to silk tulle. It is the chain-link fence of netting.

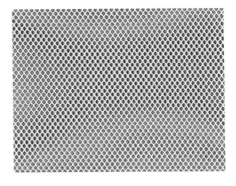

⬆ Heavy net, which is known to theater costumers as cape net, gives lots of body with next to no weight.

## Batting

Batting provides a padding that makes velvets and furs feel even more luxurious. Select silk, cotton, or wool batting. Polyester batting tends to shed over time.

*tip* **RAYON EMBROIDERY THREAD**
Fine rayon machine-embroidery thread is a good substitute for silk thread for hand-basting and similar prep tasks. It does the same work and is easier to find from online sources.

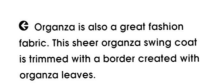

◑ Organza is also a great fashion fabric. This sheer organza swing coat is trimmed with a border created with organza leaves.

## Twill tape

Twill tape is one of the products used for stabilizing seams, roll lines, and pocket edges. Twill tape is best for heavy fabrics. Organza is more suitable for lightweight fabrics.

## Rattail cord

Rattail cord is a decorative satin cord that is ⅛" (3 mm) in diameter. A thinner version, 1/16" (1.5 mm) thick, is called mouse tail. In addition to its decorative uses, rattail cord is useful for filling piping (see page 45). It is rigid and smooth and gives finished piped edges an even thickness. It is quite inexpensive when purchased by the bolt.

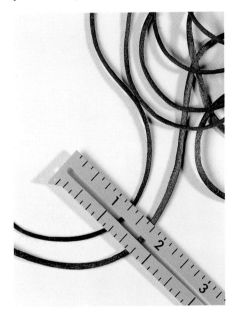

⬆ Rattail cord is a favorite of floral designers and crafters but has many couture uses, too. It's pretty, and inexpensive.

### INSTALLING HYMO THE EASY WAY

Here's an alternative to working with fusible interfacings—a method you can use in tailoring or whenever you want to avoid stiffening a seam. Use a ⅝" (1.5 cm) allowance.

**Step 1.** Cut the interfacing piece from nonfusible hair canvas or other interfacing. Also cut the interfacing piece from a thin, cheap fabric.

**Step 2.** Place the two layers together with the "cheap" fabric on the side of the canvas that will go next to the fashion, fabric. With the layers positioned this way, the cut edge of the interfacing won't leave an impression on the fabric when you press it later. Pin the layers together.

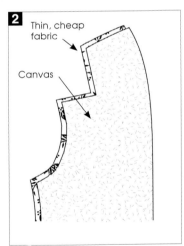

Thin, cheap fabric

Canvas

**Step 3.** Place the cut edge on the 1" (2.5 cm) mark on the sewing machine's throat plate and zigzag-stitch the pieces together. The serpentine stitch is a very strong alternative stitch. Trim the seam allowances of the interfacing close to the stitching.

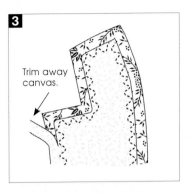

Trim away canvas.

**Step 4.** Turn the piece over. Cut the excess "cheap" fabric away from the interior of the piece, leaving the cheap fabric seam allowance around the interfacing.

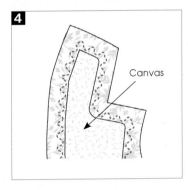

Canvas

**Step 5.** With silk thread, baste the fashion fabric to the interfacing-and-cheap-fabric unit. Basting may seem to take more time than it's worth, but the results will be far better. When you stitch this unit into the seams of the garment during construction using ⅝" (1.5 cm) seam allowance, the seamline will fall about ⅛" (3 mm) away from the cut edge of the canvas, and just the cheap fabric will be caught in the seam. The seam allowance will pad the thickness change.

# CHAPTER 2
## Equipment and TOOLS

It goes without saying that a good sewing machine and a serger are essential tools in today's sewing room. However, this equipment is not the total setup. You also need a good iron, because good pressing can save bad sewing, or bad pressing can kill a good garment. There are other tools that will make the work you do much easier and more efficient. (And they are relatively inexpensive, so they will pay for themselves in time saved.) The right tools help you to achieve more polished results, which is what we all want, do we not? So, please look over this section on tools, and then put them on your "wish list."

➜ Start with the basic sewing equipment and, with the help of a few essential tools, you will soon be creating perfect garments.

# $\mathcal{P}$resser Feet and Needles

There are many new types of presser feet and needles on the market that will make quick work of most of your sewing projects. The success of a project sometimes hinges on using exactly the right foot or needle. Two seemingly similar needles, or feet, can have subtle differences that have been engineered so each gives a specific result.

## Adjustable zipper foot

The adjustable zipper foot shown in the photo at right is 1/4" (6 mm) wide and can be attached to any machine, either with the presser-foot set screw on the shaft or with an adapter.

You will come to prefer the adjustable foot for two reasons: control and flexibility. The zipper foot included with your machine does not always allow you a wide enough range of needle positions for the techniques outlined in this book. With an adjustable foot, you can control exactly where the needle is positioned in relation to the foot. You can also see exactly where the needle is and therefore you'll have better control of your stitch placement.

This foot is not used just for applying zippers. It's easier to sew a welt pocket (see page 89) with the adjustable zipper foot than with the regular presser foot. You will also appreciate this foot for piping (see chapter 4) and lined patch pockets (see page 79). You'll need a 1/4" (6 mm) foot for the piped pockets and piped buttonholes techniques outlined in chapter 4, but you can work other methods with a slightly wider foot.

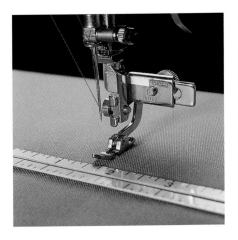

⤴ This generic adjustable zipper foot was inexpensive, but it has paid for itself a thousand times over in time and effort saved.

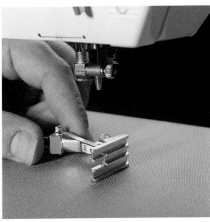

⤴ The 3-groove pintuck foot is not just for heirloom stitches; it has proven to be a useful tool for other types of sewing, too.

## 3-groove pintuck foot

When used with a double needle, this foot makes a great pintuck. The 3-groove pintuck foot is also the foot for making "Rolled Hem on Sheer Fabric" (see page 31) and "Thin, Neat French Seams" (see page 33) in chapter 3. With practice, you can install invisible zippers with this foot, too.

## Double needles

Double needles are available in a variety of sizes and are labeled with two numbers. The first number indicates the distance between the needles. This distance must correspond to the width of the central channel in the pintuck foot you're working with. The second number indicates the size of the needles themselves. Experiment with the different needle sizes available to choose the right needles for your purpose.

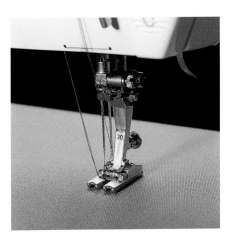

⤴ The double needle (also called a twin needle) is a specialty item that will work on most of today's machines.

# $\mathscr{P}$ressing Tools

After a good sewing machine and a serger, the next most important piece of equipment in your sewing room is a really good iron. There are a number of very good household irons on the market, but if you really want to go to town with pressing, get an industrial iron that has a gravity-feed water supply. Gravity has no moving parts! This iron is all about getting a volume of steam on demand.

Also look for an iron with weight. Purchase the heaviest iron you can manage—because of its composition, a heavy iron holds heat longer than a lighter-weight one does. Although a lightweight iron is easier to hold and lift, the heat retention is just not there. Nothing is more frustrating than having to wait for the iron to heat back up for more steam.

➲ Most people think the iron is the only necessary pressing tool, but having the full complement will improve the look of your work.

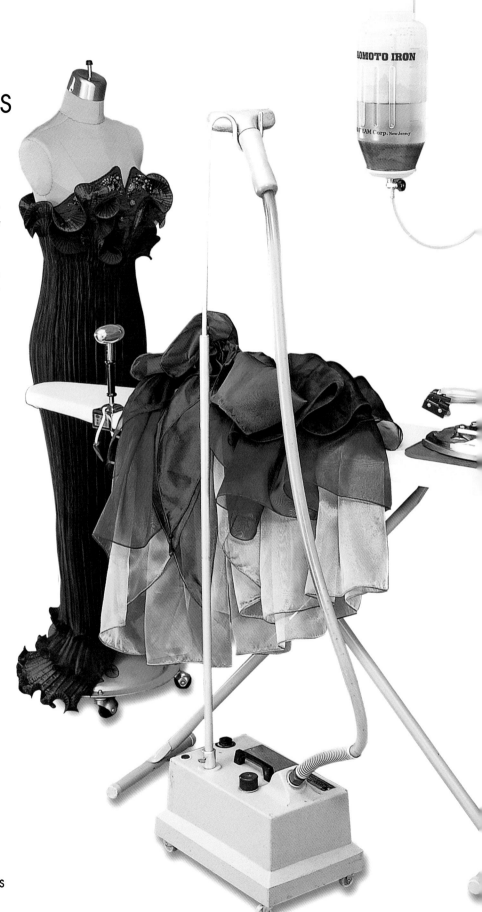

## Steamer

An industrial steamer with a heated water tank and a nozzle on a long tube is a very useful tool, and it is normally found in clothing stores. It is great for shaping a project with steam, because the steamer's nozzle is flexible and lighter in weight than an iron. A steamer comes in handy, especially when making millinery or doing other work that requires a constant stream of gentle steam—for example, when working with velvet. The steam from the ports of an industrial iron can sometimes flatten the velvet's nap, but a constant, gentle source of steam will not. You can purchase a small, handheld steamer very inexpensively (about $20) at many general merchandise stores; these will work if you don't do much steaming.

For a low-cost substitute steamer, visit a thrift store and purchase an inexpensive teakettle. Buy a length of dishwasher hose at the hardware store. Tape one end of the hose to the spout of the kettle. Fill the kettle with water and put it on the stove to boil. Wrap a hot pad around the other end of the hose to protect your hands and, voilà, you've got a steamer! When you're finished with your steaming, you can make a cup of tea!

## Puff iron

This device, also known as a pressing egg, looks like a steel egg on a post. It clamps to your pressing table and has a high/low temperature switch. If you wish to regulate the temperature more precisely, you can purchase one of the devices sold in crafting catalogs that is used to regulate the heat on wood-burning tools. The puff iron makes quick work of puffed sleeves, millinery, smocking, and ruffles.

## Pressing table

Have this table built for your studio, and you'll soon find that you cannot live without it. The table is 38" (96.5 cm) high, and the pressing surface is 24" by 60" (61 by 152.5 cm). Pad the top with cotton batting and cover it with a canvas cover that is printed with a 1" (2.5 cm) grid. The large pressing surface enables you to press a full 60" (152.5 cm)-wide fabric easily.

Underneath you can build a shelf for pressing tools. Attach cup hooks on the side to hang seam rolls, brushes, and other supplies. Mount a plug strip with an on/off switch on the side of the table. You can plug the iron and the light over the table into the strip. The little red on/off light on most irons is sometimes too subtle to see. If you see the light on over the table, you'll know the iron is still on!

**THE PRESSING SURFACE**
The best pressing surface is wood covered with cotton. This surface draws the steam and heat through the piece itself for more effective pressing. The Teflon covers on the market reflect heat and steam and produce inferior results.

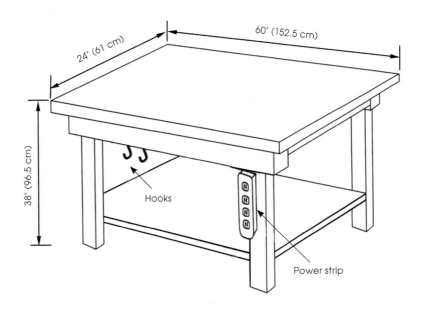

24" (61 cm)

60" (152.5 cm)

38" (96.5 cm)

Hooks

Power strip

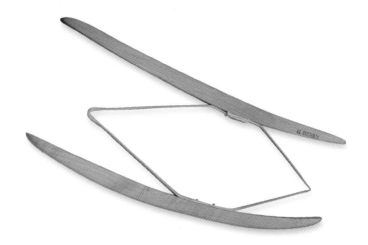

## Seam rolls

Make your own seam rolls, the ones sold commercially are too soft. Pressing with a hard seam roll produces a flat seam that will almost disappear. Closet rod dowels are best, although half-round hardwood molding works nicely, too. Cover one dowel in cotton drill for smooth fabrics, cover another in wool flannel for wools, and cover a third in mohair velvet for velvets and other napped fabrics. Hang your seam rolls from the side of your pressing table to store them.

## Sleeve boards and other pressing boards

A sleeve board is very helpful for pressing many types of difficult areas. They are available from a tailor's supply or in the notions department of fabric stores. Having a variety of smaller pressing boards that can sit on the pressing table will give you more flexibility in pressing different-sized pieces. They are all made of wood, lightly padded, and covered with cotton drill.

## Pressing ham

Purchase the regulation model, but cover one side with mohair velvet.

## Sleeve shapers

These are not essential but really nice to have for the final pressing of a jacket. These shapers are curved wooden bows separated by leaf springs. The bows are compressed and then inserted into the sleeves where they expand to the shape of the sleeve. You can then steam the sleeves to "set" them.

## The horse

The horse is a helpful tool for production sewing. As I pin the pieces, I drape them over one end of the horse to prevent creasing. When I've finished pinning, I wheel the pieces over to the machine for sewing. As I sew them, I lay them on the other end of the horse. From there, it's easy to transport them back to the pressing table.

⟳ A sleeve shaper inserted into a sleeve to support pressing won't feel the heat the way your hand would.

Make the top from a Sono tube, 12" 30.5 cm) in diameter and about 4' (1.2 m) long. Sono tubes are cardboard forms used for poured concrete footings; you can buy them at a builder's supply. Cover the tube with a matte-finished fabric to keep the pressed fabric from slipping off the surface. The tube is supported on two uprights that measure at least 4' (1.2 m) long.

◖ The point presser/clapper (sitting on the sleeve board), the seam roll, the pressing ham, and the variations on the point presser and ham are the bare minimum of pressing tools you should have in your workroom.

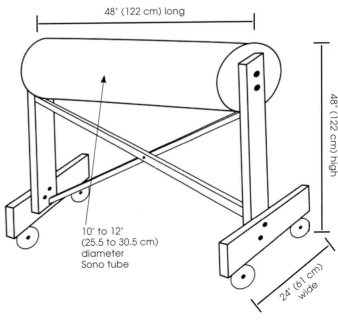

48" (122 cm) long

48" (122 cm) high

10" to 12" (25.5 to 30.5 cm) diameter Sono tube

24" (61 cm) wide

# Marking Tools

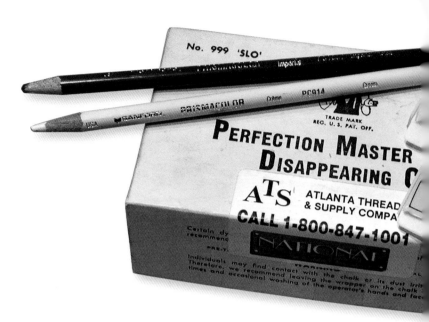

Marking tools are just as important as pressing tools, and they can make the difference between something that looks polished and professional, and something that looks like an unmade bed. Cutting corners when marking will make more work later on as well; it is really a false economy. Along with the tracing wheels, chalk wheels, and dressmaker's carbon papers that are normally in the sewing studio, here are some of my favorites that perform consistently.

## Artist's pencils

I like either the Berol Prismacolor or Schwan Stabilo pencils for marking fabrics that will be concealed by a lining. These pencils make permanent marks, so I don't use them if the garment is unlined and the marks will show, or if the fabric is sheer.

**ACCURATE MARKING** *tip*

If you're never bothered marking seamlines on your project pieces, try it. It's not at all a waste of time—you'll have much-improved results!

↑ Artist's pencils and disappearing chalk

## Disappearing chalk

You can purchase Slo-999 chalk (by Perfection Master Disappearing Crayons) from a tailor's supply or through a sewing notions company. This product disappears in 90 hours or sooner with a bit of steam. Because this chalk is air- and water-soluble, the higher the humidity, the faster it disappears. Work fast on rainy days!

Disappearing chalk won't leave oil spots on silk or residue on satins or taffetas. The only disadvantage is that, like clay chalk, this type of chalk also needs to be sharpened to create a crisp line and will break when dropped. The good news is that the dropped and broken pieces can be pounded into powder and put into the container of a chalk wheel—solving both problems at once!

## Pounce pad

This tool is borrowed from the sign-painting world, and the House of Lesage in Paris uses a variation for marking embroidery. The high-tech version of this pad costs about $10 at sign shops and art supply stores. You may wish to have two of them—one for light-colored powder and one for dark. If you prefer a lower-tech tool, put cornstarch into a clean white tennis sock and knot the end. When the sock is not in use, store it in a plastic bag.

To use a pounce pad, first use your sewing machine, with the needle unthreaded, to pierce holes in your paper pattern wherever you want to place chalk marks. Then lay the paper pattern onto the fabric and rub the pounce pad over it. The powder sifts through the holes in the paper, marking the fabric. (At the Atelier Lesage, in Paris, dark powder is "fixed" to the fabric by spraying the powder with denatured alcohol.)

## Dual tracing wheel

Many European patterns are drafted without seam allowances. Instead, sewers add seam allowances to the fabric with the dual tracing wheel and carbon paper. This tracing wheel consists of a handle and two detachable wheels mounted on pegs. The wheels run parallel to each other, so you can guide one along a stitching line, and the other will make a parallel cutting line. There are different holes that the wheel pegs plug into, so you can adjust the distance apart that they sit. Clover makes a good one.

This marking method is very accurate because both the seamline and the cutting line are marked onto the fabric at the same time. Sometimes, seams are stretched or eased before sewing, and this makes the width of the seam allowance change. If a piece were then just sewn with the standard $5/8$" (1.5 cm) mark on the machine, the seamline would not be accurate. After using this marking method for a while, you'll see that it produces more accurate results in all your sewing.

## Hera marker

A tracing wheel can distort or damage the surface of some fabrics. When working with sheer or delicate fabrics, substitute a hera marker, which functions like a thumbnail and makes an indentation or crease in the fabric. The hera marker is a plastic device about 6" (15 cm) long that is a handle with a curved end that is narrowed like a blade (see photo below). This blade is blunt, like a thumbnail edge. Used either alone or with carbon paper, it's also good for creasing paper or taffeta when heat is not desired.

↻ A hera marker, pointed and smooth tracing wheels, beading needles, and fine rayon machine embroidery thread are the minimum in marking gear to have on hand.

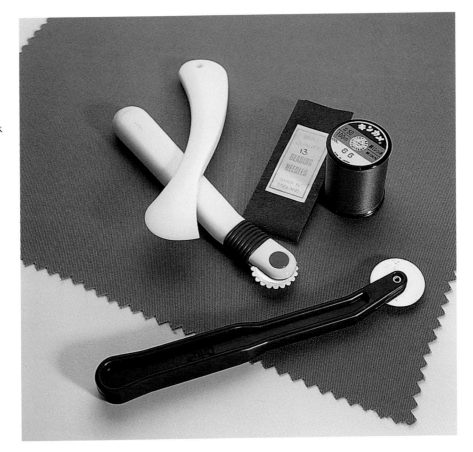

Make sure you have all the gear you need to suceed.

# $\mathcal{O}$dds and Ends

In addition to my standard shears, rotary cutter, seam ripper, and sewing threads, I've found the following various small things to be exceptionally useful in my workroom.

↑ Tailor's point scissors (top) and appli-qué scissors (bottom)

## Small scissors

Along with the usual complement of shears for cutting fabric, the tailor's point scissors and appliqué scissors are good to have on hand. Tailor's point scissors (at the top in the above photo) are 4" to 5" (10 to 12.5 cm) long and have thick spines along the back of the blades. They cut easily through many layers of fabric and, because the tips of the blades will not be forced out of alignment by thick fabric, can clip right into a point.

↑ Stiletto and stitch picker

Another feature of tailor's point scissors is that one blade is a knife edge and the other blade is a bevel edge. The knife edge enables you to get the blade point through fabric easily—for example, when you're opening up welt pockets. Once inside the pocket, you turn the scissors over, so the bevel edge blade is on the bottom. The bevel edge won't catch as readily on seam allowances, which makes grading and opening welt pockets easier to do. Once you get used to work-ing with this scissors, you'll wonder how you lived without it.

Appliqué scissors (at the bottom in the photo) have what looks like a pelican bill on one blade. This flat blade pushes aside the fabric that is not cut when trimming appliqués. This action is also helpful when grading seams because the pelican blade pushes aside the seam allowance that is not being cut. Another good feature to look for when shop-ping for scissors is the combination of a forward fulcrum and thick spines along the backs of the blades. This combination provides strength, power, and control when cutting.

## Stiletto and stitch picker

A stiletto and stitch picker is a useful tool to have handy at your sewing machine. It will save your fingers. The non-pointed end, which looks like a flat fingernail clipper, is for pulling out stitches that you can't get hold of with your finger-nails. The pointed end of the tool is traditionally used to steer fabric through the sewing machine, to avoid sewing through your fingers.

↑ Fine silk sewing threads

## Fine threads

When basting interlinings to fashion fabric, or when basting interfacings, you want to work with fine silk thread. Regular sewing thread will leave marks on the fabric when you press. Fine silk thread won't. When basting eveningwear fabrics, such as satins and charmeuse, work with a number 10 beading needle, too. The fine needle and thread will en-sure that there are no marks in the fabric when you remove the basting.

Fine rayon embroidery thread or fine-spun nylon thread are good substitutes for silk thread. Polyester, however, can melt if the iron is too hot. If you aren't sure how your basting thread and fabric will work together when sewing and pressing, experiment on a piece of scrap fabric before you commit.

G A stiff stencil brush easily removes chalk marks.

## Housepainter's brush

A basic housepainter's paintbrush is good for general dusting and brushing of fabric. I buy what they call the "chip" brush at the paint store. ("Chip" equals cheap.) Mine is 3" (7.6 cm) wide, but choose whatever width you prefer. You will want to cover the metal fitting on this brush, too, just as you did for the stencil brush.

## Electric shavers

There have been times that I've snagged a fabric in a highly visible place, and these tools have saved my bacon. They are just what they look like—men's electric shavers. The ones in the photo are battery-operated, and I bought them at a drugstore. The round-headed model is really inexpensive (about $5), but it cuts a little more coarsely than the more expensive square-headed model.

I prefer face shavers to the fabric shavers you buy at the fabric store, but you should have one of those, too. Fabric shavers, which remove pilling from fabrics, are a little too aggressive sometimes, and they can leave a scuffmark on certain types of fabrics.

Face shavers are a little more precise in removing fuzz and stray ends of thread, so you can even use them on satin (I have) without leaving a mark.

## Wire-bristle brush

A brass wire-bristle brush will save your behind if you inadvertently put shine on your fabric. The wire bristles are fine enough that they will brush off shine without abrading the fabric. The brush will also lift the nap on brushed fabrics such as wool melton.

## Stencil brush

There are times when you need to brush chalk marks out of fabrics that are resistant to releasing chalk—like flannels, for example. A stencil brush, which you can get at either a paint store or an art supply store, is ideal for this job. The bristles are dense and cropped to form a flat surface. This bristle configuration is what gets the powder out of fabrics.

I've also seen this brush work miracles with vintage felt hats. It gets out all the old dust and also gives the nap a lift.

As you can see in the photo, I've covered the ferrule (metal fitting) with fabric. I do this to avoid snagging the fashion fabric with the rough metal of the brush. Learn from my mistake!

⌂ Brass wire-bristle brush

➋ Electric shavers are great little tools for shaving pilling and fuzz.

With a fully equipped workroom,
you're all set to sew!

# CHAPTER 3

# Edge and Seam
# FINISHES

The edge and seam finishes presented in this chapter sprang from my desire to have neat, clean, polished results on transparent fabrics. The classic couture ways of making these seams are nice, but to my taste, not as strong as I feel is needed in the modern world.

I invented the technique of making a rolled hem and French seam with the serger and sewing machine while I was making the silver tissue lamé cape shown. This fabric was actually silver metal thread woven with silk, so it required as little handling as possible during construction. The overlap seam (see page 35) is strong, flat, and makes a sheer garment look like a line drawing.

➲ This gorgeous silver metal and silk tissue lamé cape was created with the cool techniques for sewing sheer fabric explained in this chapter.

# Rolled Hem on Sheer Fabric

To make this rolled hem, I first sew a tiny rolled hem with my serger, and then fold and press that edge twice to the wrong side of the project; I secure this hem with a small zigzag stitch sewn on my standard sewing machine with a pin-tuck foot. So to complete this technique, you will use your sewing machine, your serger, and a 3-groove pintuck foot. Set up your serger for the 3-thread rolled hem, referring to your machine manual. Rayon embroidery thread works well for most fabrics, but monofilament is best for metallic fabrics.

**SERGER SETTINGS**

*Cutting Width: 1*
*Stitch Length: 1.0–1.5 mm*
*Differential: 0.7 mm*

*The serger stitch length regulates the fluidity or rigidity of the hem. The basic rule of thumb is the longer the stitch length, the more fluid the hem.*

**Step 1** Serge the edge with the 3-thread rolled hem. If you are finishing a curved edge, machine-ease the edge first to control the bias (see page 172). Then, serge over the ease stitching, making sure you don't cut off the stitching while serging.

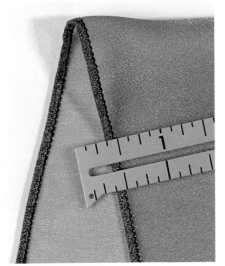

⬆ This rolled hem is easy to do, and it provides a polished hem on sheer fabrics.

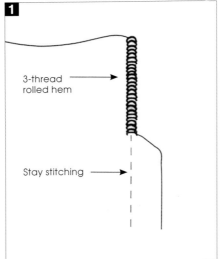

1

3-thread rolled hem

Stay stitching

*tip*

**SECURING THE CHAIN**
If the serger chain wants to fall off the edge (this sometimes occurs when hemming a curved or bias edge), increase the cutting width so there is more fabric to roll into the hem.

**Step 2** Press the rolled edge toward the wrong side of the piece. Fold and press the edge again so the serged rolled hem is completely concealed.

**Step 3** Attach a 3-groove pintuck foot to the sewing machine. Move the needle position so it sits over the left toe or edge of the center groove of the pintuck foot (some machines call this a half-left position). Set the machine as shown in the box below.

### SEWING MACHINE SETTINGS

*Stitch:* Zigzag
*Stitch Width:* 0.6–0.9 mm
*Stitch Length:* 0.9–1.2 mm

**Step 4** Place the pressed rolled edge, face up, in the center groove of the pintuck foot, with the body of the piece to the left. Catch the left fold of the fabric with the right-hand swing of the needle while sewing, securing the hem. The narrow width setting for the zigzag stitch allows the stitching line to blend with the fold, producing an almost identical appearance on both sides of the rolled hem.

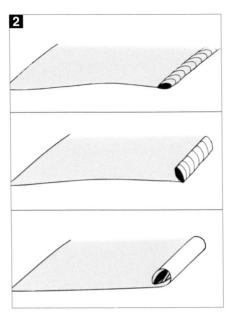

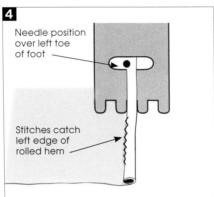

Needle position over left toe of foot

Stitches catch left edge of rolled hem

*tip*

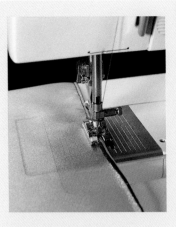

This is what the work looks like properly positioned in the machine for a rolled hem.

*tip*

**TENSION HELPS**
To get the tightest roll, pull the fabric slightly to the left as it passes under the foot. This tension will snug the fabric around the serger chain while it is being stitched into place.

# 𝒯hin, Neat French Seam

French seam with the sewing machine and serger. Now doesn't that title sound like a contemporary music composition? Once you have mastered the rolled hem, the French seam will be easy to understand. This seam is narrow and strong enough to secure a sleeve in an armhole, as long as the cut edges are not too deeply curved. The finished seam looks like a pintuck, so you can stitch it on the outside of the garment to add a design element. Rayon embroidery thread works well for most fabrics, but monofilament is best for metallic fabrics.

I have found that working with both the serger and the sewing machine I can create the thinnest and strongest French seam possible. Having a thin, strong seam is key, especially in garments that are fitted, because the strain on a seam in a fitted garment can pull apart other seams.

You will need the favoring technique to sew this seam. Favoring is the process of shifting the seamline slightly on one or both pieces so that you can manipulate the seam allowance in a special way or reposition the seam without changing the size of the finished work.

A French seam is actually two seams, with the second one enclosing the seam allowance of the first one. For my method, when you sew the second seam, the fabric will be wrapped around the serged edge of the first seam, so you need to shift the position of the first seam closer

to the edge on one piece, or "favor" that piece, in order to have enough seam allowance left for the wrap of the second seam. When you sew the second seam, the original seamlines of the two pieces will align. Try the following steps on a scrap, and you'll see how neatly it falls into place. The drawings below shows what the first seam looks like if it hasn't been offset to favor one piece, and what it looks like when it has been offset.

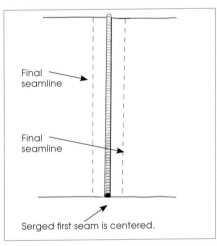

Final seamline

Final seamline

Serged first seam is centered.

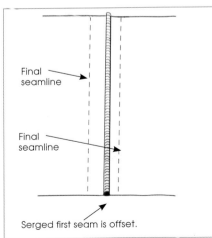

Final seamline

Final seamline

Serged first seam is offset.

⬆ A serged and straight-stitched French seam on transparent fabrics is the absolute epitome of polished sewing.

## SERGER SETTINGS FOR FRENCH SEAM

*Cutting Width:* 1
*Differential:* 0.7 mm
*Stitch Length:* 1.2–1.5 mm

## SEWING MACHINE SETTINGS FOR FRENCH SEAM

*Stitch:* Zigzag
*Stitch Width:* 0.6–0.9 mm
*Stitch Length:* 0.9–1.2 mm
*Thread:* Rayon embroidery thread or monofilament (for metallic fabrics)

**Step 1** With wrong sides together, favor the upper layer of fabric by ¼" (6 mm) and pin.

**Step 2** If the seamlines fall on the bias (as with gored skirts or gored capes), stay-stitch at ⅜" (1 cm), while machine-easing slightly. The staystitching keeps the bias from stretching and dragging down the lines of the garment.

**Step 3** Sew a 3-thread rolled hem on the serger, placing the cut edge of the upper (favored) layer on the serger's ⅝" (1.5 cm) mark.

**Step 4** Open the seam and press the chain of the rolled hem toward the under layer.

**Step 5** Fold the fabric over the rolled hem chain with right sides of the fabric together. To fold the fabric in this manner, you need the favoring. Without it, the seam would sit to one side of where it is intended in the design.

**Step 6** Flip the piece over and with the 3-groove pintuck foot on the sewing machine, set the machine needle position to half-left.

As with the rolled hem, the zigzag stitch falls over the fold making both sides of this seam appear the same. The finished effect is like a pintuck, not a seam.

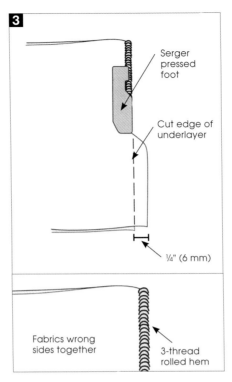

3

Serger pressed foot

Cut edge of underlayer

¼" (6 mm)

Fabrics wrong sides together

3-thread rolled hem

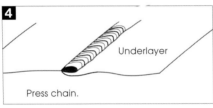

4

Underlayer

Press chain.

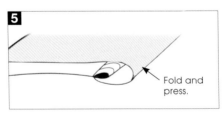

5

Fold and press.

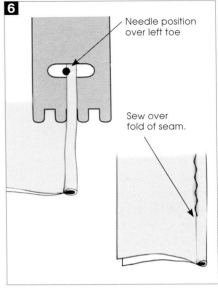

6

Needle position over left toe

Sew over fold of seam.

# Overlap Seam

In my quest for narrow but strong seams for transparent fabrics, I figured out this overlap seam. It's strong and narrow, and it works for straight seams and curved seams on transparent fabrics such as organza, chiffon, and georgette—which means you can use it to set a sleeve into an armhole. For this technique you sew the fabric to tissue patterns that you make, then cut them out, and then overlap the pieces while still on the tissue. When you lay the fabric over the patterns, both must be right side up. So in step 1, be sure to make a pattern for every piece you need: left and right sides and full patterns for any pieces that you would usually cut on the fold. Use a separate piece of tissue for each piece so that you can align the grainline with the fabric later. Make sure anything you have two of is arranged as a pair—you don't want to end up with two left sleeves— and mark the pieces "right side up."

I first used this seam on an organza bolero jacket I made for a customer who was going to the Nobel Prize award ceremony banquet. Apparently, where the royal family of Sweden will be present, one can't have an exposed armpit— which means no strapless dresses, unless something is worn over them. (I guess that an exposed armpit once caused some sort of international incident. The things one learns in this business!)

⬆ The overlap seam is a perfect seam for sheer fabrics, decorative and useful at the same time.

**Step 1** To begin, draft your pattern pieces, drawing the stitching lines onto tissue paper; leave 3" (7.5 cm) between pieces if more than one fits on your tissue. If you are using a commercial pattern, leaving this space between pieces, trace the seamlines, grainlines, and any matching marks onto tissue paper; don't trace the cutting lines. You want to see the stitching lines when constructing this seam.

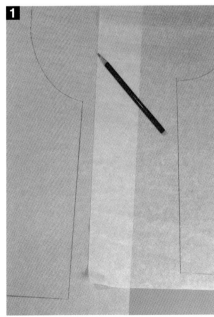

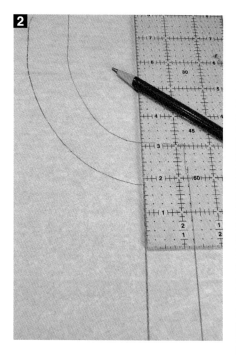

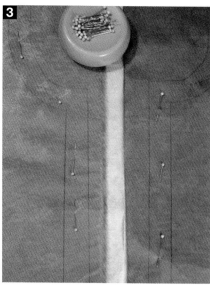

**Step 2** Then, using a grid ruler as a guide, draft on 1¼" (3 cm) seam allowances; this marks your cutting lines.

**Step 3** Lay the fabric onto the tissue and pin. If there is a right side to your fabric, be sure to place it face up over the tissue. In the photos, I used two different colors of fabric—lilac (on the left) and pink (on the right)—to make the process clearer.

**Step 4** With a standard ¹/₁₀" (2.5 mm) straight stitch, sew the fabric to the tissue along the stitching lines.

**Step 5** When the stitching lines are all sewn, cut the fabric and the tissue together along the marked cutting lines.

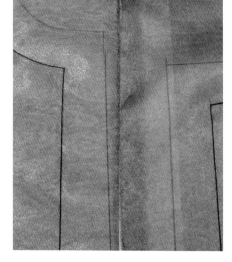

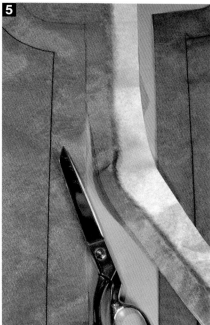

**Step 6** Now, place the first two pieces you plan to sew together right side up with the seam allowances side-by-side. Working on the left piece (the lilac side), tear away the tissue from the seam allowance, keeping the tissue connected to the body of the piece.

**Step 7** Lay the left piece (lilac) onto the right (pink) piece. Align the two stitching lines and pin together, one right on top of the other.

**Step 8** With the same straight stitch, sew along the previous stitching lines to join the two pieces together.

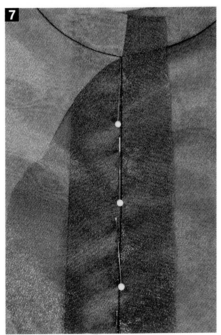

**Step 9** Tear away the tissue from the seam allowance on the pink side.

**Step 10** Now the two pieces are overlapped and sewn together, with the seam allowances facing opposite directions, as shown.

**Step 11** On the pink piece, lift the tissue away from the seam or tear a little bit away along the seam. Fold over and press the pink seam allowance against the pink side of the seam. After they're pressed, you can see that both cut edges point in the same direction.

**Step 12** With the pink seam allowance side up, edgestitch $1/8$" (3 mm) away from the fold, onto the seam allowance. You will be sewing through both seam allowances and the pink side of the seam.

**Step 13** Turn the work over. Lift the lilac seam allowance and fold and press it against the lilac side of the seam. The cut edges of the seam allowances will be facing opposite directions again.

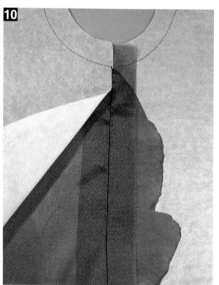

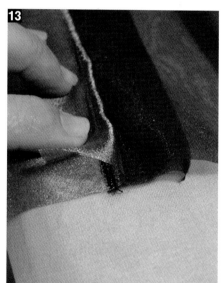

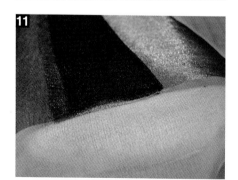

**Step 14** Edgestitch ⅛" (3 mm) away from the fold, onto the lilac seam allowance. Here is the finished edgestitching.

**Step 15** This next step is one I do for safety, to make the seam really secure. Set the machine for a three-step zigzag (or a serpentine stitch, as shown in the photos) at a stitch width of 1.8 mm and stitch length of 0.75 mm. Sew, centering the stitching over the seam.

**Step 16** Finally, cover all of the stitching you've done so far with satin stitch, set to a width of 3.8 mm.

**Step 17** Very carefully, trim away the lilac seam allowance, really close to the satin stitching.

**Step 18** Turn the work over and, again, very carefully trim away the pink seam allowance, close to the satin stitch. You're done!

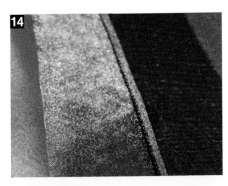

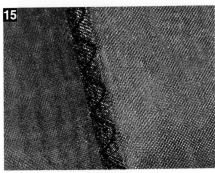

# Foolproof Lapped Zipper

The mere mention of installing a zipper frightens many people. Because I am a lazy guy, and want to just slam a zipper in without worry, I have devised this installation method, which is quick and has two advantages: the zipper teeth are offset from the seamline so they're well hidden, and the zipper tape is attached to the outside of the garment by hand with a tiny pick stitch, which is nearly invisible. After you understand it, the process will take you a maximum of ten minutes for a skirt or slacks.

Start with a zipper that's longer than the opening you want. You'll install it with the excess length at the top so you avoid dodging around the zipper slide when stitching, which always makes the garment look homemade. When the zipper is installed, you'll cut off the excess and add a new top stop. My prejudice when choosing zippers is to use metal ones in important garments because metal zippers last longer. Save the plastic zippers for things that will receive one season's wear. (I always seem to melt the plastic ones when pressing!)

When you're sewing this, remember that the underlap is the seam allowance closest to your body when you're wearing the garment and doesn't show; the overlap is the section that covers the zipper. You need wider seam allowances for this technique, so read the directions before you cut out your garment.

The lapped zipper is a classic application used mainly on tailored skirts. This version sets the zipper farther away from the seamline behind a deeper-than-usual overlap, so it hides nicely when closed.

**STRESS REDUCTION**

Make your skirt openings 9" (23 cm) long, rather than the 7" (18 cm) called for in most patterns. The fullest part of the hips generally falls 8" to 9" (20.5 to 23 cm) below the waist. A 7" (18 cm) zipper will strain the end of the opening, causing the zipper to fail.

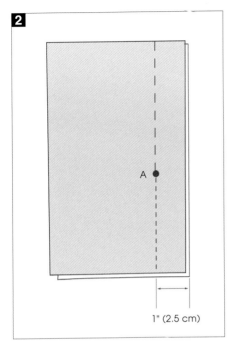

**2**

A

1" (2.5 cm)

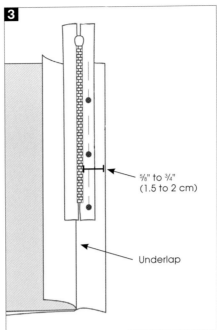

**3**

⅝" to ¾"
(1.5 to 2 cm)

Underlap

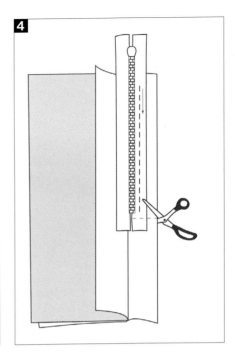

**4**

**Step 1** Before cutting your pattern, redraw the seam allowances all along the seam where the zipper will be installed to make them 1" (2.5 cm) wide.

**Step 2** Using a long machine basting stitch, sew the zipper opening closed along the seamline; remember the allowance is 1" (2.5 cm). When you reach the place where you want the bottom of the zipper to be, stop and back tack (A on the drawing). Close the rest of the seam with a regular stitch length.

**Step 3** With the fabric still right sides together, lift and fold back the top seam allowance, leaving the bottom allowance extending. (You can choose which way you want the zipper to lap; these drawings show a left-over-right lap when the garment is on the body.) Place the zipper face down with the teeth on the extending allowance, which will be the underlap when you're finished. Put the zipper bottom stop (the metal guard at the bottom of the zipper opening) just above point A and align the outer edge of the teeth ⅝" to ¾" (1.5 to 2 cm) from the cut edge of the seam allowance, as shown. Notice I didn't mention the edge of the zipper tape—where that falls is immaterial. Pin the zipper tape to the extending allowance.

**Step 4** Sew the zipper tape to the seam allowance using a zipper foot. Stop stitching at point A (just below the bottom zipper stop). Clip through the seam allowance (but not the tape) just below the stop, stopping the cut in line with the seam just sewn through the tape.

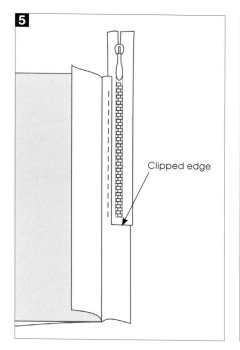

**5**

Clipped edge

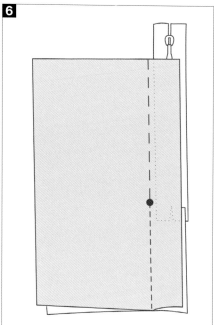

**6**

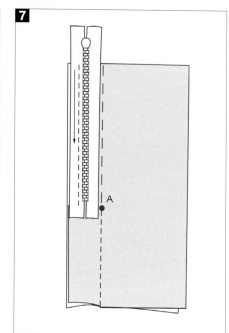

**7**

A

**Step 5** Turn the zipper right side up, folding the extending allowance along the seam and tucking the end of the tape behind the clipped edge, as shown, then edgestitch the fold. This keeps the fashion fabric from jamming in the slide of the zipper.

**Step 6** Fold down the top seam allowance again, enclosing the zipper (like closing a book). There is no favoring or other manipulation needed.

**Step 7** Flip the work over. Stitch the loose edge of the zipper tape to the loose seam allowance, stopping at point A.

*tip* **REVERSAL OF FORTUNE**
If you install a metal zipper wrong side up by mistake, simply remove the top stops, slide off the slider, reverse it, and slide it back on.

## PICK STITCHING

A pick stitch is a tiny handmade backstitch spaced at ¼" (6 mm) intervals and used for the last step of attaching a lapped zipper or anywhere you'd like special, small topstitches. The pick stitch is quick and easy, and screams couture! A good silk buttonhole twist is nice for pick stitching—the shine of the twist against the fabric, with the tiny stitches, is very attractive.

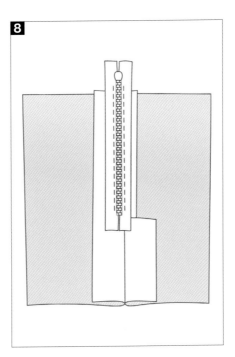

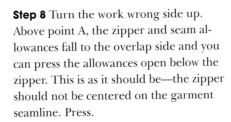

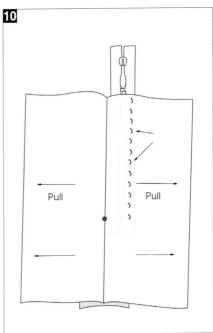

**Step 8** Turn the work wrong side up. Above point A, the zipper and seam allowances fall to the overlap side and you can press the allowances open below the zipper. This is as it should be—the zipper should not be centered on the garment seamline. Press.

**Step 9** Turn the work right side up. To finish the overlap, pick-stitch along the zipper, attaching the tape to the fashion fabric on the overlap side, as shown in the drawing in step 10. Draw a chalk line first to guide the stitches. If the zipper falls on a curve (such as a hip curve), hold the work in a curve when stitching to build in the shape.

**Step 10** Once the pick stitching is finished, remove the machine basting that closes the seam in the zipper opening and press. Pull the work in the direction of the arrows when pressing. This counteracts the natural tendency for the overlap to roll out and makes the overlap lie flat.

**Step 11** Pull the zipper slide down, opening the zipper, and then cut off the excess zipper tape and teeth at the top. Make a stop stitch at the end of the teeth on one side (or zigzag over the teeth) to keep the slide from accidentally slipping off before you add the waistband.

# CHAPTER 4

# Piping

Piping is a detail that I've used from the very beginning of my business. I like the opportunity it provides for introducing color or texture at an edge of a design, and I also like the substance it gives to a seam. I've also discovered over the years that using piping makes for easier pocket and buttonhole openings. Further, it allows one to install linings into pieces in a way that hides hand-stitching.

Piping can also be part of the design of a garment, separating different sections such as yokes and bodices in interesting ways. It can be used in straight lines or curves, in single or multiple rows.

➲ Classic single piping of dark avocado green creates a subtle, contrasting edge to this opulent black wool bolero jacket.

# Basic Piped Seams

I almost always make my own piping from rattail cord (see page 17) covered with bias strips (see page 170) of a fabric that enhances whatever I'm sewing; the techniques in this book assume you are doing the same. Understanding a few tricks for working with piping will make your work look really polished and sophisticated. Even if you routinely use piping, read this section so you see my technique for the basic process—you'll need to understand it for my other piping techniques.

Single piping is a classic design detail seen in many styles of clothing and also in furnishings. The design potential of using piping is endless. It can add definition to seams on a simply cut garment, making the seams an ornament. The colors and patterns used to make the piping can add texture and color to a design. Structurally, the piping gives more body to a seam, which gives a garment more shape. Also, piping can hide hand-stitching, so linings and facings look polished. People sometimes avoid piping, believing that it is too difficult to install, but with the information that follows, you will get good results whenever you decide to use it!

To make piping, you'll work with a bias cover—the bias strip of fabric that wraps the material that fills the piping. The fill can be any number of materials—from rattail cord to yarn—and a variety of sizes. Rattail cord is a satin cord, about ⅛" (3 mm) thick, which is often used for decorative work. It's made of rayon and comes in a variety of colors.

As a general rule, for greater stability, instead of inserting the piping at the same time you sew two pieces of fabric together, stitch the piping to the seamline of one piece of fabric and then sew the seam that joins it to the other piece of fabric. Use the ¼" (6 mm) adjustable zipper foot for this basic technique. When you sew the cover around the cord and also when you sew the piping to the first piece of fabric, the needle will be just a little bit farther from the cord than when you sew the final seam, which will be snug up against the cord. This means there won't be any extra stitches peeking out in your finished work. I call these two needle positions "position 1" and "position 2." They describe the relationship of the needle to the zipper foot, not specific needle positions on your machine.

⬆ Piping is a useful detail that gives definition to a seam and substance and structure to the piece.

## POSITION 1 & 2
In these instructions, position 1 and position 2 describe the relationship of the needle to the foot, not specific needle positions on your machine.

**Step 1** Cut bias strips of fabric 1" to 1¼" (2.5 cm to 3 cm) wide. Stitch the bias strips together to make a long continuous strip (see page 170).

**Step 2** Put the zipper foot on your sewing machine, placing it to the right of the needle, and adjust it so that the needle is as close to the inside of the foot as possible (this position is position 1). You'll use position 1 when making piping and when stitching the piping to one piece of a project after basting and before the second piece is attached. Remember, position 1 is used on anything that is not a final seam.

**Step 3** Fold the bias strip over the rattail cord as shown, and sew next to the cord with a stitch length of at least ⅛" (3 mm). Shorter stitches will stiffen and draw up the seam.

**Step 4** Place the project piece to be piped right side up. Place the piping on top, along the edge to be piped, with the fill oriented toward the inside of the project piece. Set a seam gauge to ⅝" (1.5 cm) (or whatever your project seam allowance is). Using the seam gauge as a guide, position and pin the piping to the project; snug the gauge tight against the piping so that the final seam will be closer to the fill than the stitches holding the cover around the fill. Once the piping is pinned in place, hand-baste onto the fabric, then sew it on the machine with the needle still in position 1.

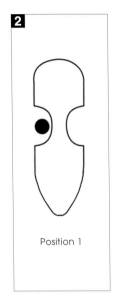

Position 1

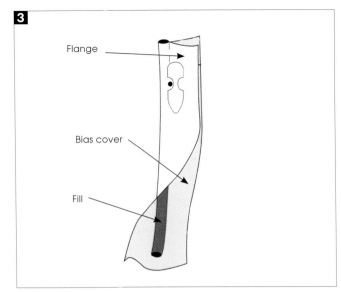

Flange

Bias cover

Fill

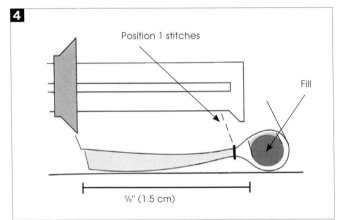

Position 1 stitches

Fill

⅝" (1.5 cm)

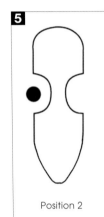

Position 2

**Step 5** Place the first project piece right side down over the second, aligning the cut edges on the piped seamline; pin along this seamline. Place the work in the machine with the first piece on top so you can see the stitches that secure the piping. Move the zipper foot to the right slightly so that the needle is just outside the left edge of the foot. In this position, the needle will be closer to the rattail fill when you sew, causing the previous lines of stitching to fall into the seam allowance. This adjusted position is position 2. Sew the final seam with the foot in position 2. To prevent the seam from drawing up, use a stitch that is ⅛" (3 mm) or longer. Remember, position 2 is for final seams only.

# $\mathcal{P}$iped Corners

Piped straight seams are easy, but piped corners cause problems for most folks. Here are some tricks you will find helpful when piping outside corners; my technique for piping inside corners is on page 49.

## Outside corners

Outside corners are most common on vest points and collars. It's easier to make an outside piped corner than a piped inside corner.

**Step 1** When hand-basting the piping to the seamline (yes, basting!), baste along one side to the corner and then measure the seam allowance depth from the other direction to determine where to pivot. Mark the piping with a marking pen at the pivot point. Make a hand tack with needle and thread on the right side of this mark to secure the piping in place.

**Step 2** Clip the piping seam allowance at the mark and pivot the piping around the corner. Push back the piping, to the right. The piping will roll back on itself, which is exactly what you want. If it doesn't, the corner will be round instead of square.

**Step 3** Make a hand tack with needle and thread on the left side of the pivot mark. Continue basting.

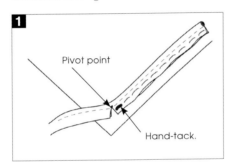

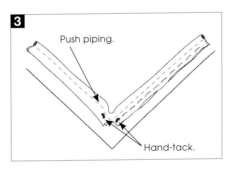

⬆ The contrasting piping defines the point at the small of the jacket back. The beading on the piping is applied after the facings are installed.

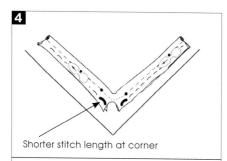

Shorter stitch length at corner

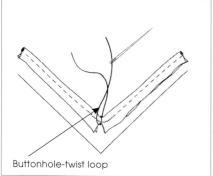

Buttonhole-twist loop

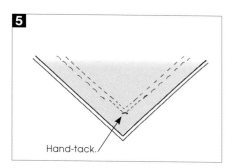

Hand-tack.

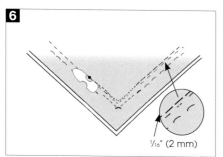

1/16" (2 mm)

**Step 4** To sew on the piping, place the zipper foot in position 1 and sew, stopping about 1/2" (1.3 cm) before the pivot mark. Shorten the stitch length to 0.3–0.5 mm and continue stitching to the pivot mark. The piping will have to be rolled out of the path of the needle as you stitch. Pivot the fabric slightly and stitch one or two stitches across the corner, pivot again, and stitch for another 1/2" (1.3 cm). Lengthen the stitch back to normal and continue stitching the piping in place.

If the corner is fairly sharp, to make turning easier later, stitch a loop of buttonhole twist to the corner of the piping, after you've finished the machine stitching. Be sure not to stitch this thread into the seamline.

**Step 5** To sew on the lining or facing, pin the pieces right sides together and baste. Baste the corner with tiny stitches while pinching the fabric together at the machine-stitching line and at the same time rolling the piping so the machine-stitching line is in contact with the fabric on the other side. This maneuver is done by feel. Baste along the stitching line to the pivot point and make a tack stitch.

Push the piping back into the piece on the other side. Remember, we let the piping roll onto itself in step 2. Now it will want to push out of the side that isn't basted. Baste, making sure the layers are properly aligned. Finish basting.

**Step 6** Sew the final seam with the zipper foot in position 2. Shorten the stitches about 1/2" (1.3 cm) away from the corner, making sure the foot is securely against the piping (the rattail is firm enough and will provide a good guide). The stitching line will be a scant 1/16" (2 mm) inside the original machine-stitching line. Stitch across the corner and up the other side as described in step 4.

**Step 7** Clip the corner, grade the seams, and prepare to turn the piped corner right side out. Turn, pulling the loop of buttonhole twist, if you added one, to turn the corner crisply. Remove the buttonhole-twist loop from the seam before pressing.

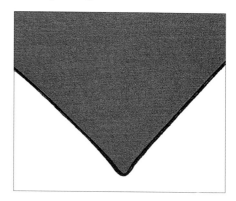

⬆ Crisp outside corners on piped seams are the mark of a well-made piece. Achieving them is easy when you follow the information set out here.

## Inside corners

You can't easily turn piping around an inside corner, but that doesn't matter! An inside corner is a logical place to begin and end piping, while also creating a very nice detail.

**Step 1** At the inside corner, measure from the cut edge and mark the corner seamline on the right side of the project. Along one side of the corner, baste the piping to the seamline as usual but extend the piping end 1" (2.5 cm) beyond the corner onto the body of the piece. Trim the seam allowances to $1/8$" (3 mm) for approximately 2" (5 cm) from the end of the piping.

Baste the piping in place all around, ending up at the opposite side of the corner. Trim the seam allowances at this end the same way. Baste so that the stitching lines at the ends are $1/4$" (6 mm) away from one another, adjusting as necessary to keep them centered.

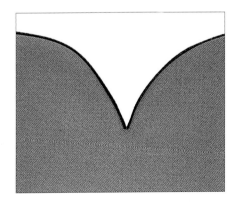

⌃ A piped inside corner looks especially good at the back of a neckline.

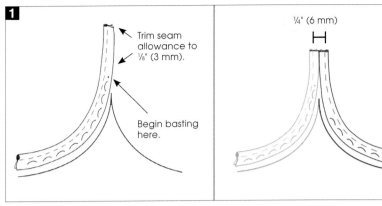

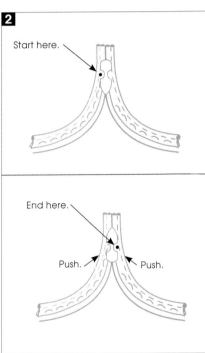

**Step 2** Start stitching with the zipper foot in position 1 and a stitch length of 0.3–0.5 mm. Sew for $1/2$" (1.3 cm), then lengthen the stitches to $1/8$" (3 mm) to attach the piping all along the seamline. Then, $1/2$" (1.3 cm) before you reach the opposite side of the corner, shorten the stitches again to finish. While you are sewing the final $1/2$" (1.3 cm) of piping, push the two ends of the piping together, so the zipper foot uses the beginning end as a guide. The zipper foot will follow the beginning portion of the piping, and push away the end portion so it stitches exactly $1/4$" (6 mm) away—the proper space needed between these two rows of stitching.

**Step 3.** With right sides together, and the piped piece on top so you can see the previous stitching, pin the facing or lining to the piped piece; put the zipper foot in position 2. Start stitching with the short stitches for ¹/₂" (1.3 cm), then change to your normal stitch length to attach the rest of the piece. Shorten the stitches again at the other end, ¹/₂" (1.3 cm) before the stopping point.

**Step 4** Thin the piping ends so the fill will not get caught in the seam: First place a pin through the piping to keep the fill from pulling out completely. Then measure from the end of the piping to the seamline to find out how much fill to remove. Peel the bias strip back while holding the fill, exposing the fill. Cut off the fill at the measured distance and pull the bias strip back over the cut end.

Then, clip the seam allowance at the corner into a "triangle" on both layers. Working with a bodkin, pull the ends of the piping to the wrong side through the corner opening, between the ends of the seams. Turn the piece right side out.

**3**

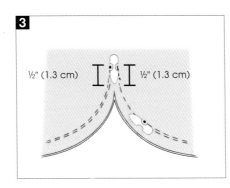

½" (1.3 cm)  ½" (1.3 cm)

**4**

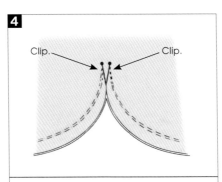

Clip.  Clip.

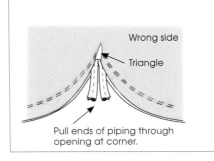

Wrong side

Triangle

Pull ends of piping through opening at corner.

**5**

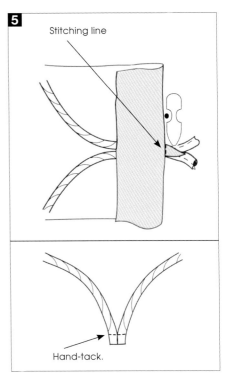

Stitching line

Hand-tack.

**Step 5** To finish the inside corner, stitch across the base of the "triangle," catching the ends of the piping in the stitching. To ensure a crisp, sharp angle, hand-tack the pipings at the corner, pulling the pipings together.

**SHORT STITCHES**    *tip*

You stitch with short stitches at the corners and the beginning and end of inside piped corners for two reasons. First, the short stitches reinforce the seam for clipping later. Second, they keep the seam from drawing up, as a back tack would, and if needed you can remove the stitches one at a time to ensure an even corner.

# Complex Piped Seams

Sometimes there is a complex piped seam within a garment piece, such as a sharp angled seam, that is difficult to construct in the usual way. You see these seams usually for yokes on garments, but they can also be used for complex princess seams, or for adding dramatic cuffs to sleeves. Here's an alternate method of construction for those situations. Because this is basically an overlap seam that creates a raised effect on the work, it is best to install the piping on whichever piece you want to lay on top—on the piece you want to sit on a higher plane.

**Step 1** Baste the piping to the right side of the fashion fabric and stitch with the foot in position 2 (this is a final seam). After the piping is sewn in place, trim and clip the seam allowances and press them onto the wrong side of the piece.

**Step 2** With both pieces right side up, lay the piped piece on top of the seam allowance of the adjacent piece. Baste together the two pieces, aligning the cut edges of the seam allowances.

**Step 3** With an edge stitching foot, stitch in the ditch along the seam that joins the piping to the piece, as shown in the photo at right.

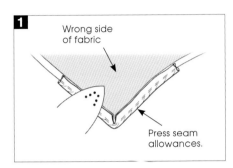

1  Wrong side of fabric

Press seam allowances.

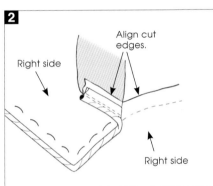

2  Align cut edges.

Right side

Right side

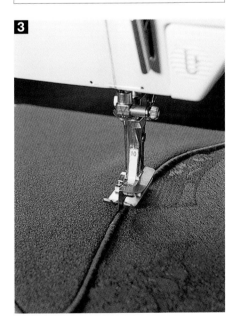

3

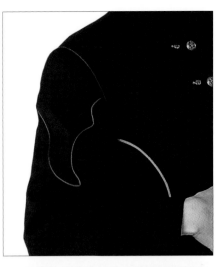

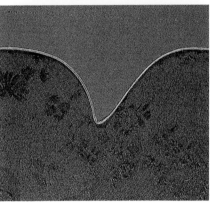

⬆ The intricate shapes of a complex piped seam add drama to a piece.

# Double and Triple Piping

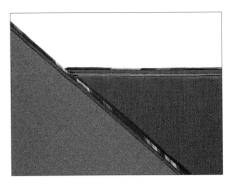

A single row of piping is nice, but you can really enhance an edge with double and triple rows of piping. You could make multiple pipings simply by stitching a number of pipings together, but some curious people might pull them apart, see the stitching lines, and say, "Tsk, tsk!" Here's a better approach: make one piece of piping, sew another bias strip to it, and then fill the second piece; if you want a third piece, you add it in the same way. When the pipings are assembled as one unit, then you sew them to the project in the usual way. This multiple piping can go around most curves, but not angles or sharp corners. Remember this limitation when planning your project.

If you want to use multiple piping all around a piece in such a way that the ends will butt—say, at the wrist of a wide sleeve or at the edge of circular piece—try to plan the design so some embellishment will cover the join. If this won't work for your design, overlap the ends, pull out the stitching that holds the strips together, and join the individual bias strips, cutting the fill to butt and folding one end of each cover strip over the other one (just like piping a pillow). Then stitch final seams in the order of construction.

**Step 1** Cut and stitch together bias strips for each layer of piping in the usual manner, but cut the strips at least 1¹/₂" to 2" (4 to 5 cm) wide. You can always trim later, if necessary. The first row of piping will be on the outer edge of the project; the last one you add will be nearest the fashion fabric.

**Step 2** Make the first layer of piping following the instructions in "Basic Piped Seams" (see page 45), with the zipper foot in position 1.

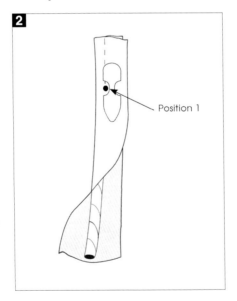

Position 1

⊙ Double and triple piping are more architectural than single piping is. These piping styles make terrific edges on garments that you'd like to give a three-dimensional enhancement.

**Step 3** Lay the second-layer bias strip right side up and center the finished piping on top. Sew them together with the zipper foot in position 2, as shown (this is a final seam). By making the layers of piping in this way, the stitching line will not show in the finished piece.

**Step 4** To fill the second bias strip, turn over the sewn-together strips and rotate them so the first piping is on the left; lay another piece of fill next to the first one, and fold the second strip over it. Put the zipper foot back into position 1 and sew next to the second fill.

**Step 5** To add a third layer of piping, follow steps 2 and 3 but stitch next to the second piping. You can add even more layers, but adding more than three pipings hampers flexibility, so curves are not as easy to negotiate. Straight lines are best in a piece with more than three pipings.

**Step 6** When you are ready, sew the piping to your project in the usual way, with the piping face-down to the right side of the fabric and the zipper foot in position 2. It is essential to hand-baste the piping down in this instance.

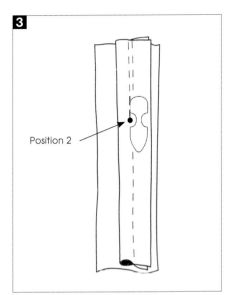

3

Position 2

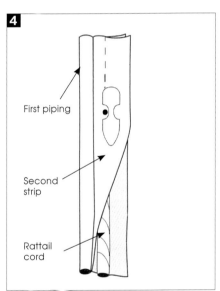

4

First piping

Second strip

Rattail cord

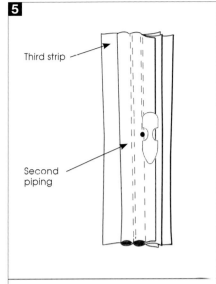

5

Third strip

Second piping

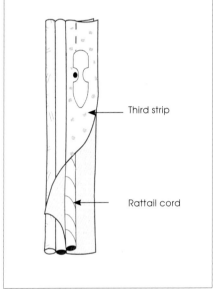

Third strip

Rattail cord

## Lining for multiple piping

Now, you might ask, how do you put a backing onto this? There are two methods, both of which involve handwork. The dreaded handwork, you ask? Really, sometimes handwork is faster and easier than using the machine!

With the first method, you cut the facing, with the seamline moved outward, to match the extra width on the piped edge created by the multiple rows. The rule of thumb is to add an extra $1/8$" (3 mm) for each additional row of piping (remember, the outer row of piping extends beyond the lining, as usual). Press under the seam allowance along the seamline and then pin and hand-stitch the fold to the outermost row of piping.

The second method involves adding piping to the facing (or lining), too, but with one less row of piping than on the outer piece. For example, if you are using triple piping, pipe the facing with a double piping. Then hand-sew this to the outer piece. The outermost row of piping on the piece will form a point, as shown in this drawing of a cross section of the edge.

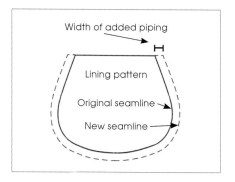

Width of added piping

Lining pattern

Original seamline

New seamline

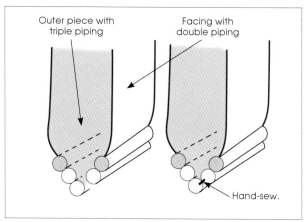

Outer piece with triple piping

Facing with double piping

Hand-sew.

# $\mathscr{P}$iped Buttonholes and Pockets

Now that you have an understanding of piping, you can take on the piped buttonhole and pocket next. You can make horizontal or vertical openings, or even put them on the bias. The openings can be decorative rather than functional, if you like. To make them decorative, follow "Completing a Piped Buttonhole," page 59, through step 11, then simply sew them shut by hand. If you wish, you can embellish the outer ends of the piped openings with a combination of decorative buttons and metal ends for a very beautiful look.

For these techniques, you will use the 1/4" (6 mm) adjustable zipper foot, and you will quickly see why you simply must have this particular foot. You can use the same fashion fabric for the piping as is used for the garment, or choose a contrasting fabric, as I've done for the piece in the photos here. Follow the directions for single piping, page 45, cutting the bias strips 1 1/4" (3 cm) wide. For each buttonhole or pocket, you need two pieces of piping, each 1 1/2" (4 cm) longer than the opening.

The construction method for the piped buttonhole and piped pocket is the same through the steps for sewing on the piping, so these directions cover both together to that point, and then each is continued separately. You'll see I demonstrate this on a small piece of fabric that represents the garment piece, so don't be confused by the edges in the photos.

The rule of thumb for pocket opening size is that it should be no less than 6" (15 cm) in length. This amount allows room for the hand to get into the pocket. I prefer an opening of 6 1/2" or 7" (16.5 or 17.8 cm) for women's garments and 7 1/2" or 8" (19 or 20 cm) for men's. Mark the placement for the buttonhole or pocket opening on the right side of the fashion fabric (on the body of the garment, not the facing) with thread basting or with chalk that can easily be brushed away. Refresh your memory of zipper foot position 1 and position 2 (see page 45). You'll use position 1 to sew the piping and position 2 for all construction steps that follow.

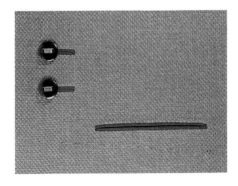

⬆ The piped pocket and buttonhole are classic details on tailored garments for both men and women.

⬆ Multicolored piping turns a very simple jacket pattern playful but chic. Gold jewelry findings on the ends of the buttonholes add a touch of shine

If you are making a buttonhole in a garment that has heavy interfacing (such as Hymo) under the area of the buttonholes, make the buttonholes in the fashion fabric layer only, before you attach the interfacing to the project. Trust me: If you sew piped buttonholes or pockets through the interfacing, they will never press flat.

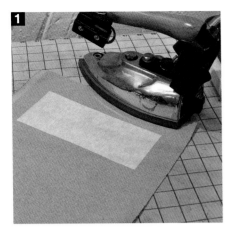

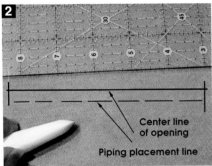

Center line
of opening

Piping placement line

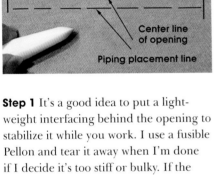

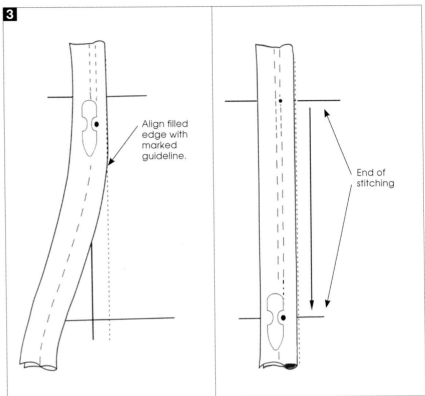

Align filled
edge with
marked
guideline.

End of
stitching

**Step 1** It's a good idea to put a light-weight interfacing behind the opening to stabilize it while you work. I use a fusible Pellon and tear it away when I'm done if I decide it's too stiff or bulky. If the opening is on the bias, use a double layer of organza, running the lengthwise grain parallel to the opening.

**Step 2** On the right side of the fabric, mark the center line of the buttonhole or pocket opening and mark the ends of the opening across it. Next, mark a parallel line a scant ¼" (6 mm) (more like ³/₁₆" [5 mm]) away on one side of the opening line. This is the piping placement line.

**Step 3** Cut two pieces of piping, each 1½" (4 cm) longer than the marked opening. Lay one piece over the marked opening, aligning the filled edge with the placement line, lapping the cut edge over the center line, and letting ³/₄" (2 cm) extend at each end for finishing. Pin or baste if you wish.

With the zipper foot in position 2, sew the piping on between the end marks. For a pocket, start stitching at one end with a short stitch length of 0.3–0.5 mm. Stitch for ½" (1.3 cm) with the short stitches, then lengthen the stitches to 1.0–1.2 mm. Shorten the stitches again ½" (1.3 cm) before the end and stop on the end mark. For a buttonhole, use only the short stitch length.

**Step 4** Trim the seam allowance of the sewn-on piping to $1/8$" (3 mm). Trim the seam allowance on the second piece of piping to $1/8$" (3 mm).

**Step 5** Shift the needle to the opposite side of the zipper foot, placing it in position 2. With the filled edge facing away from the first piece of piping, place the second piece of piping under the foot, pushing it as close to the first piping as possible—the allowances will overlap. Starting at the same end as before, pull the free end of thread from the first piping across the second, as shown, so you can see exactly where to begin sewing.

**Step 6** Lower the foot between the two pipings. Continuing to push them together, sew on the second piece of piping; the foot will push them apart the required distance. If you cross the second piping slightly onto the first, as shown in the photo, the foot will push it into the correct position. Stitching in the same direction will prevent the pocket from looking "twisted" when it's finished.

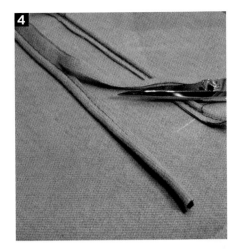

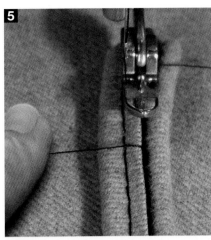

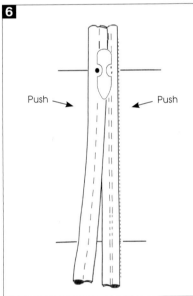

Push → ← Push

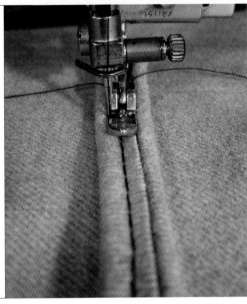

**PARALLEL PIPING**

As you stitch along the second piping, keep the right edge of the foot tight against the first piping. The foot is exactly the width of the opening and will keep the two pipings parallel. Shorten and lengthen the stitches as in step 3.

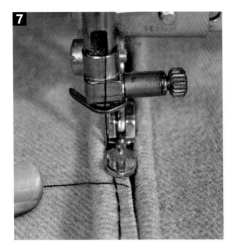

Open bias cover to end mark.

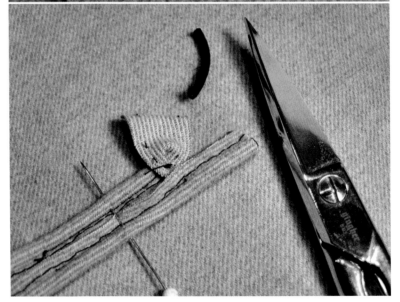

**Step 7** At the opposite end, pull the free end of the thread from the first piping over as a guide for where to stop sewing.

**Step 8.** After you've sewn on both pieces of piping, you need to thin the ends so they don't make the ends of the opening bulky. Put a pin through the piping, as shown, to make sure you don't pull the fill out completely. Then, at each end of each piece, take out the stitches in the bias cover and hold it open where the piping is not sewn to the garment. Pull the fill gently and cut if off; the remaining fill should be slightly shorter than the length of the pocket or buttonhole.

If you inadvertently pull out the rattail —not to worry! Stitch the end of the rattail to the eye of a tapestry needle— end to end—and thread the rattail back into piping.

At this point, the construction methods for the piped pocket and piped button-hole begin to differ. Follow the specific steps that follow to finish each.

## Completing a piped buttonhole

**Step 1** Turn the work over. Cut the opening in a long X, forming triangles of seam allowance, as shown. Be sure to clip exactly up to the ends of the stitching—if you wimp out you'll have puckers at the end of the opening.

**Step 2** Fold the seam allowance to the wrong side through the opening, making sure the ends of the opening are square by laying the piece flat, right side up. Baste the filled piping edges together with silk thread. The silk thread won't leave marks when pressed.

**Step 3** Lay the work wrong side up on a seam roll, with the buttonhole opening lengthwise on the roll, as shown. Press. This approach ensures that seam-allowance impressions won't mar the appearance of the fashion fabric.

**Step 4** To finish each end of the buttonhole, fold the garment fabric back onto the opening, perpendicular to the opening line. Pull the triangle of fabric over the ends of the piping, as shown, and, with the zipper foot in position 2, stitch very short stitches across the ends. Because of the zipper foot, the line of stitching falls right where it is wanted, without disturbing any of the parts.

*tip*

**TRIMMING**
If you've trimmed the fill from the piping ends and clipped correctly, the fabric in the opening will fold back just where it should.

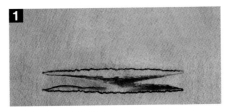

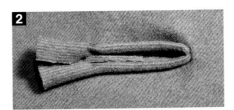

*tip* **PERFECT ENDS**
Make sure the piping pieces don't overlap at the end of the opening. Pull the ends of the piping apart just before stitching, and then release.

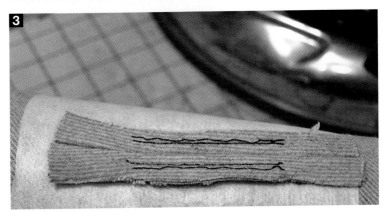

**Step 5** Turn the work over. The button-hole should look like the photo.

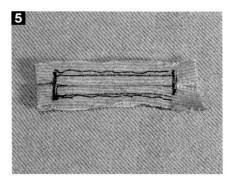

**Step 6** If you are making a garment with canvas interfacing, now's the time to attach the interfacing to the wrong side of the fashion fabric piece. If your garment doesn't have canvas interfacing, you can go right to step 12.

**Step 7** Turn the work right side up and insert a pin through each corner of each buttonhole.

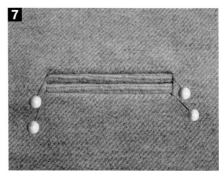

**Step 8** Turn the work wrong side up. Mark where each pin comes through the canvas. Then draw a rectangle a hairline ($1/16$" [2 mm]) outside the marks.

**Step 9** Cut the canvas along the marked outline, making a little window.

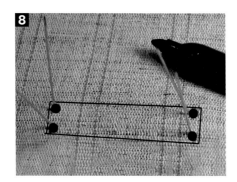

**Step 10** Pull the piping seam allowances through the window. Make sure the edge of the window floats unimpeded behind the seam allowances. Cut a larger window if there is any buckling.

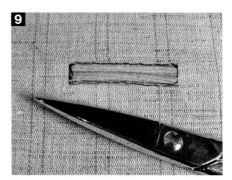

**Step 11** By hand, whipstitch the seam allowances loosely to the canvas.

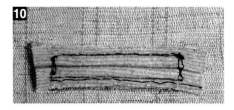

**Step 12** After the facings are sewn to the garment, pin a small piece of organza to the right side of the facing behind each buttonhole.

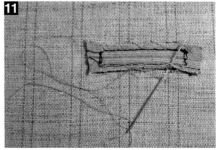

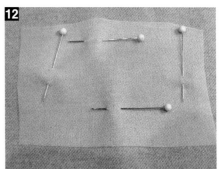

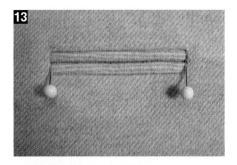

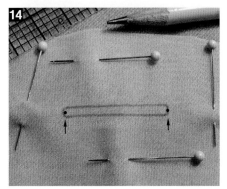

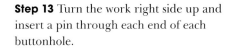

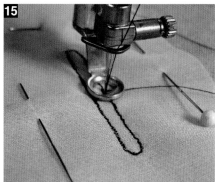

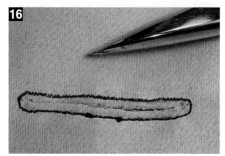

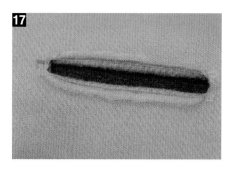

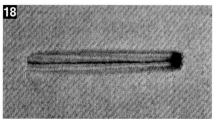

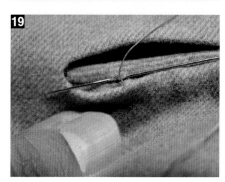

**Step 13** Turn the work right side up and insert a pin through each end of each buttonhole.

**Step 14** Turn the work over and mark the points where the pins come through the organza. Then draw an oblong $^{1}/_{8}$" (3 mm) wide between the pins.

**Step 15** Put a darning foot on the sewing machine and drop the feed dogs. Lift the facing away from the garment and use a free-motion stitch to sew the marked oblong.

**Step 16** Cut a slit from one end of the stitched oblong to the other end.

**Step 17** Insert the organza through the slit and smooth it against the wrong side of the facing. Press.

**Step 18** Lay the facing back into position behind the buttonhole. You've created a faced opening that frames the piping.

**Step 19** Slipstitch the facing to the buttonhole.

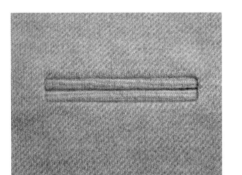

⬆ The finished buttonhole looks almost as good on the facing side as it does on the front of the garment (below).

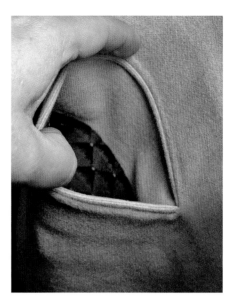

⬆ A band of fashion fabric at the top of the pocket bag back means the lining fabric won't be visible when you put your hand in the pocket or if you lean forward.

## Completing a piped pocket

The next step is to make the pocket bag. It has two pieces, a long rectangle that I make of lining fabric, which gets folded to be the bag front and back, and a small band of the fashion fabric to go right behind the pocket opening at the top of the bag back. I call this band the facing. It isn't really a facing but I can't think of a better word for it, and I need to be able to refer to it. You can see the inside of the pocket bag in the photo at right, with the facing right below the top piping, and the lining below the facing.

⬆ The buttonhole looks fabulous from the front of the garment, too.

◀ Unadorned—or trimmed with jewelry findings like the ones shown here—piped buttonholes add beautiful, surprising detail to a garment.

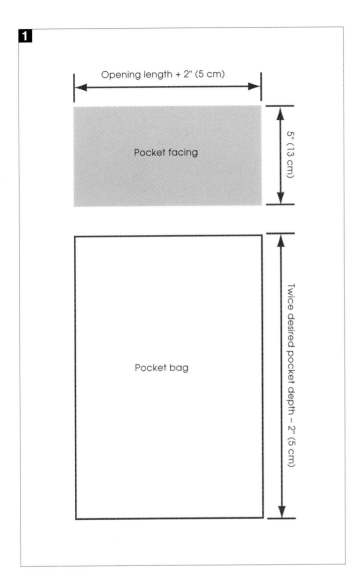

**1**

Opening length + 2" (5 cm)

Pocket facing

5" (13 cm)

Pocket bag

Twice desired pocket depth – 2" (5 cm)

**Step 1** Draft patterns for the pocket bag and the facing, as shown in the drawing at left. The drafting formulas are on the drawings, but the depth of the pocket is up to you; I usually use the length of the hand to determine the depth, but a breast pocket or pockets on a short jacket can be shallower.

**Step 2** Cut out the pocket bag and facing. Lay the garment with the piped pocket opening right side up, with the bottom edge closest to you. Lay the facing right side down on top, centering it side-to-side over the piping and aligning the bottom edge $\frac{1}{2}$" (1.3 cm) below the stitching of the bottom piping. You will sew the facing in place along the stitches that attach the top piping to the garment. Pin or baste it into position. Turn the work over. The photos show each side of the work.

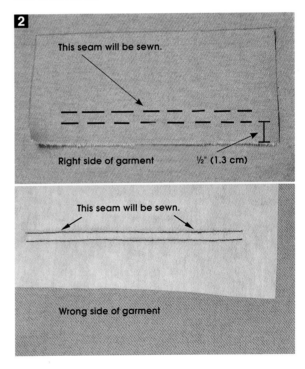

**2**

This seam will be sewn.

Right side of garment          $\frac{1}{2}$" (1.3 cm)

This seam will be sewn.

Wrong side of garment

**Step 3** Keep the garment wrong side up, and put the zipper foot in position 2. Sew again along the top piping stitching line. As you're stitching, the zipper foot will travel between the two stitching lines (and the two pipings).

**Step 4** Turn the work over.

**Step 5** Fold up the seam allowance of the facing to reveal both pipings and then pin as shown.

**Step 6** Lay one end of the pocket bag right side down over the piping, aligning it with the folded-up edge of the facing seam allowance. Pin to the garment as shown.

**Step 7** Turn the work over. Identify the bottom piping stitching line, the line the facing wasn't sewn to.

**Step 8** Shift the needle to the opposite side of the zipper foot, in position 2. Sew along the bottom piping stitching to attach the pocket bag.

**Step 9** Turn the work right side up and make sure the facing and pocket bag look like the photo; you should see only the piping seam allowances between the facing and pocket bag.

**Step 10** Cut the pocket opening between the piping stitching, as shown by the solid lines in the drawing at right. Begin in the middle of the opening and cut toward each end, cutting a long triangle at each end. From the wrong side the opening will look like the photo.

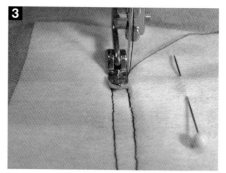

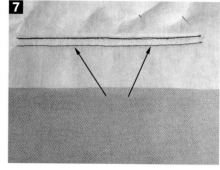

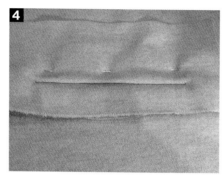

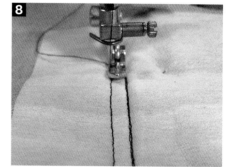

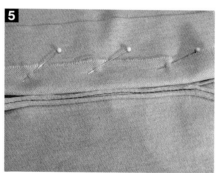

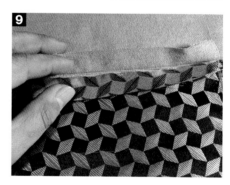

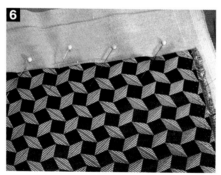

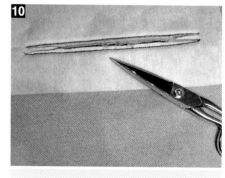

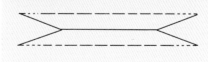

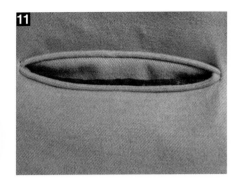

**Step 11** Insert the facing, pocket bag, and piping ends through the opening.

**Step 12** If you like, baste the opening closed with silk thread. Place the work right side down on a seam roll, with the pocket opening lengthwise on the roll, and press.

**Step 13** To finish each end of the opening, fold the garment fabric back onto the opening, perpendicular to the opening line. Pull the piping ends onto the facing, then pull the triangle of fabric over the ends of the piping, as shown, and, with the zipper foot in position 2, stitch very short stitches across the ends. Because of the zipper foot, the line of stitching falls right where it is wanted, without disturbing the placement of any parts.

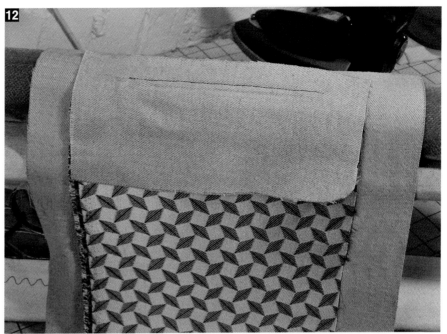

**Step 14** Turn the work over; it should look like the photo shown here.

**Step 15** With the work still wrong side up, fold up the loose end of the pocket bag and align it with the loose bottom edge of the facing, lifting the facing so you can put the two pieces right sides together, as shown. Pin.

**Step 16** Sew the pocket bag and facing together as pinned with ½" (1.3 cm) seam allowance. Press the seam allowances down, away from the facing (don't press the bottom of the pocket bag yet).

**Step 17** Turn the work over and then fold the garment up to reveal the pocket bag front. Fold a ½" (1.3 cm) pleat across the front of the bag only. This pleating is a trick to keep the bag from gaping later.

**Step 18** Press the creases of the pleat and then press a crease across the bottom of the bag. You're now ready to sew the sides of the bag closed.

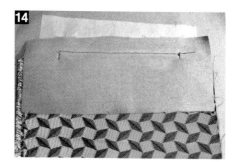

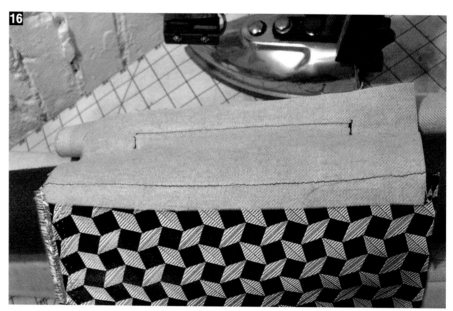

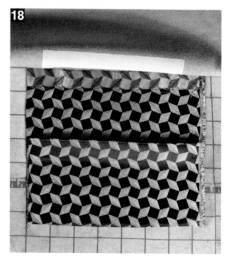

**Step 19** Keep the garment folded up, away from the pocket bag, and now fold it over at the right end of the pocket, as shown. With the zipper foot, start sewing the bag closed, stitching close to the end of the pocket opening.

**Step 20** Sew all the way around the pocket bag, rounding the corners, as shown. Square corners are more likely to attract lint.

**Step 21** Trim the edges of the pocket bag with pinking shears or finish them with a serger.

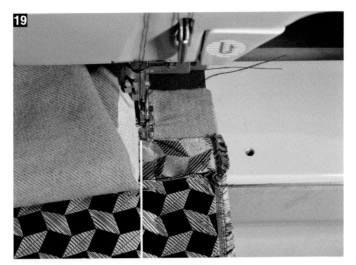

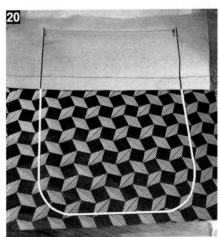

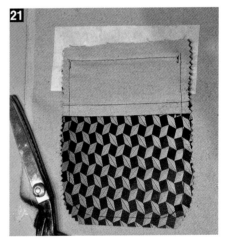

**CHECK THE DEPTH**
After pinning in step 15, the pocket bag should be 1" (2.5 cm) deeper than desired. Shorten it now if you wish.

↻ Turn the work over. Your pocket is done.

➲ Piping looks crisp and neat, and discreet. If you want to call attention to it, use contrasting fabric.

# $\mathcal{P}$iped Curved Pockets

The curved piped pocket (the "smile" pocket of Western wear) is similar in construction to the piped pocket. Use the same dimensions for the pocket opening (see page 55). Here, I demonstrate this technique on a small piece of fabric that represents the garment piece, and I've used some fusible interfacing on the wrong side to support the pocket opening. If you've never made a piped pocket (see page 63), it's a good idea to practice that process before you do this one. Once you understand how putting a pocket in a straight opening works, it will be easier to visualize the way this one goes together.

Just as for the piped pocket, the pocket bag is cut in two pieces: a long rectangle that I make of lining fabric, which gets folded to be the bag front and back, and a small band of the fashion fabric to go right behind the pocket opening at the top of the bag back. I call this band the facing. It isn't really a facing, but I can't think of a better word for it, and I need

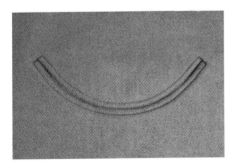

⊙ This curved pocket is a "smile" pocket! You, too, will smile when you master this versatile technique.

to be able to refer to it. You need an adjustable zipper foot for this technique, and for each pocket, you need two pieces of piping, each 1½" (3.8 cm) longer than the opening. Refresh your memory of zipper foot position 1 and position 2 (see page 45); you'll use position 1 to sew the piping and then use position 2 for all construction steps that follow.

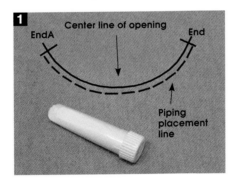

**Step 1** On the right side of the fabric, mark the center line of the pocket opening (shown as a solid line in the photo) and mark the ends of the opening across it. Next, mark a parallel line a scant ¼" (6 mm) (more like ³⁄₁₆" [5 mm]) below the curved line.

**Step 2** To make a curved design, first draft the curve of the opening and the end marks on paper or with chalk on the right side of your project so you can be sure you like it. Draw the facing and pocket bag pieces as shown. The drafting formulas are on the drawings, but the depth of the pocket can vary. I usually use the length of the hand to determine depth, but a breast pocket or pockets on a short jacket can be shallower.

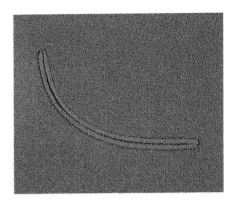

⊙ The curved pocket comes to us from Western wear, but has a completely different effect when applied to garments other than cowboy clothes.

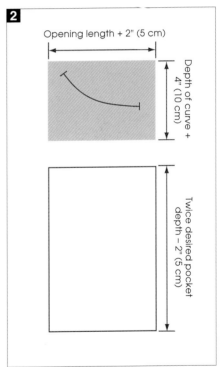

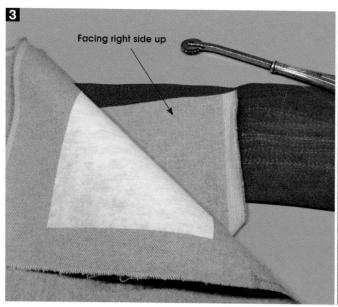

Facing right side up

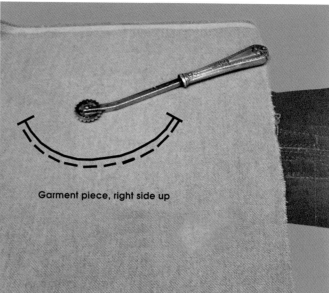

Garment piece, right side up

Marked facing, wrong side up

**Step 3** Cut the facing from the fashion fabric and the pocket bag from the lining fabric. Place a piece of carbon tracing paper carbon-side up on your table. Place the pocket facing right side up on top. Place the garment piece with the marked pocket right side up and centered side-to-side over the facing.

**Step 4** Trace the center line and end marks onto the wrong side of the pocket facing piece.

**Step 5** On the facing, staystitch the marked center line between the end marks with a $1/10"$ (2.5 mm) stitch.

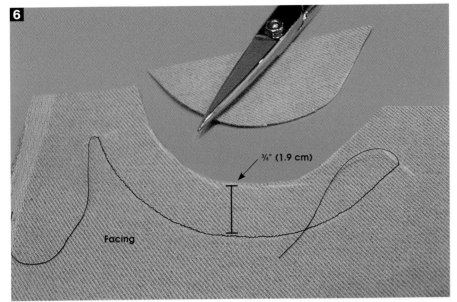

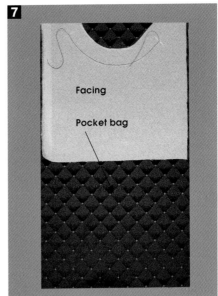

**Step 6** Mark a ¾" (2 cm) seam allowance above the line of stitching, and trim away the fabric above this marked line.

**Step 7** Lay the pocket facing onto the pocket bag. Notice where they meet at the top of the rectangle? You will align these edges later on.

**Step 8** Place the garment piece right side up and align the filled edge of one piece of piping with the marked (lower) guideline, as shown (cut edge up). With the zipper foot in position 2, sew on the piping. Start at one end mark, and sew with short (0.5 mm) stitches along the entire length of the pocket opening. Stop at the end mark.

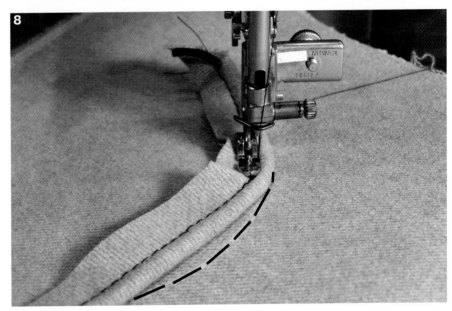

**Step 9** Trim the seam allowance of this piping to ⅛" (3 mm). Then, trim the seam allowance of the second piece of piping to ⅛" (3 mm).

**Step 10** Shift the needle to the opposite side of the zipper foot, placing it in position 2. With the filled edge facing away from the first piece of piping, place the second piece of piping under the foot, pushing it as close to the first piping as possible. Start sewing on the end mark with the same short stitches. Keep pushing the second piping toward the first piping, and guide the zipper foot along the first piping. Stop at the end mark.

**Step 11** Remove the work from the machine. It should look like the photo shown here.

**Step 12** Cut the fill out of the ends as explained in step 8 of the piped pocket (see page 58).

**Step 13** Clip the seam allowance of the pocket facing close to the curved line of staystitching, as shown in the photo here.

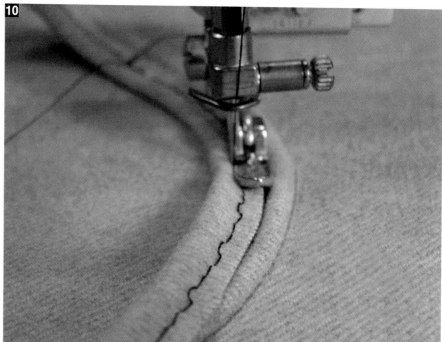

**PARALLEL PIPING**    *tip*

As you stitch along the second piping, keep the right edge of the foot tight against the first piping. The foot is exactly the width of the opening and will keep the two pipings parallel.

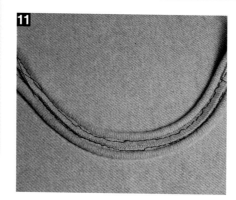

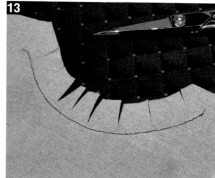

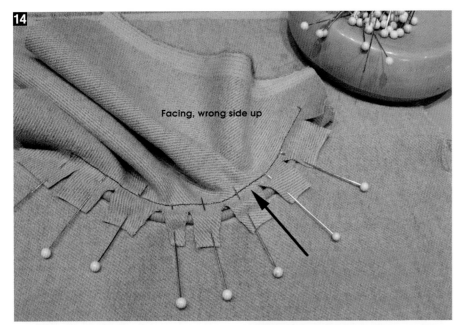

**Step 14** Pin the facing, right side down, to the piped curve on the garment, aligning the staystitching along the center line of the pocket opening (between the pipings).

**Step 15** By hand, baste the staystitched line on the facing to the pocket opening line on the garment. Remove the pins.

**Step 16** Turn over the work and sew the facing to the top row of stitching, with the needle to the right of the foot, in position 2, and with the same short stitches.

Facing, wrong side up

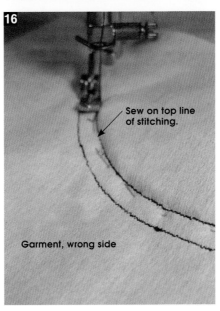

Sew on top line of stitching.

Garment, wrong side

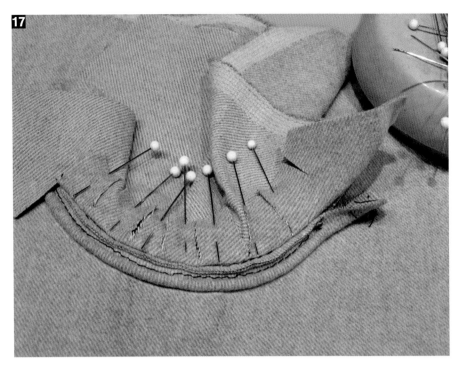

**Step 17** Turn the work over. Fold up the clipped seam allowance and pin it to the facing, so you won't catch it in the seam you'll sew in the next step.

**Step 18** Remember how the pocket bag and facing aligned in step 7? Now you'll align them that way on the garment. Lay the pocket bag right side down on the garment, with the top end over the curved piping. On the facing, fold up the straight, loose edge at each end of the curved seam, and align the top edge of the pocket bag on it. Pin the top edge of the bag to the garment over the curved piping.

**Step 19** Turn the work over and sew along the bottom curved stitching to attach the pocket bag to the garment.

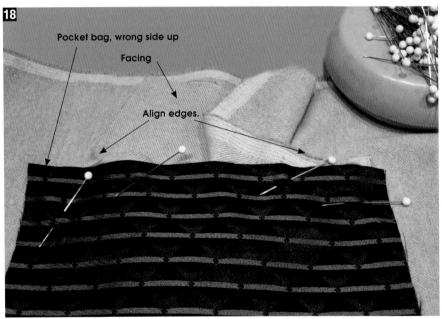

Pocket bag, wrong side up

Facing

Align edges.

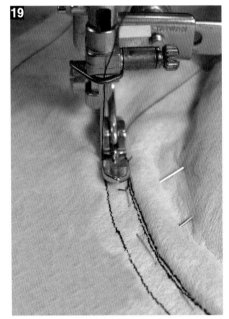

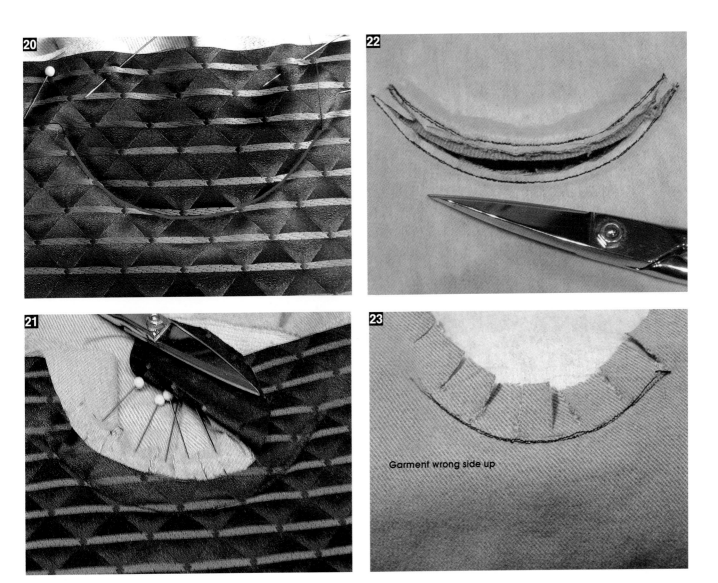

Garment wrong side up

**Step 20** Remove the work from the machine and turn it right side up. It should look like the photo above.

**Step 21** Cut away the fabric above the curved seam on the pocket bag as shown. Clip the curves of the allowance.

**Step 22** Cut the pocket opening as you would for a straight piped pocket (see "Completing a Piped Pocket," step 10, page 64), making sure there are long "triangles" at the ends.

**Step 23** Insert the facing, pocket bag, and piping ends through the opening. Fold both the facing and the pocket bag down, as they'll hang when you wear the garment. Press the seam allowances of the upper piping up and press the seam allowances of the lower piping down.

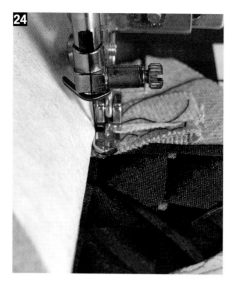

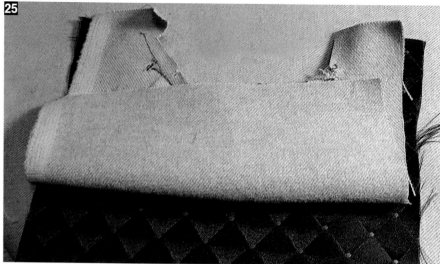

**Step 24** To finish each end of the opening, fold the garment fabric back onto the opening, perpendicular to the opening line. Pull the piping ends onto the facing, then pull the triangle of fabric over the ends of the piping, as shown, and, with the zipper foot in position 2, stitch very short stitches across the ends. Because of the zipper foot, the line of stitching falls right where it is wanted, without disturbing the placement of any parts.

**Step 25** With the work still wrong side up, fold up the bottom of the facing.

**Step 26** Fold up the loose end of the pocket bag and align it with the loose bottom edge of the facing (they will be right sides together). Pin the edges together.

**Step 27** Sew the pocket bag and facing together as pinned with ⅝" (1.5 cm) seam allowance. Press the seam allowances down, away from the facing (don't press the bottom of the pocket bag yet).

**Step 28** Turn the work over, and then fold the garment up to reveal the pocket bag front. Fold a ½" (1.3 cm) pleat across the front of the bag only (see step 17, page 66). This is a trick to keep the bag from gaping later.

**Step 29** Press the creases of the pleat and then press a crease across the bottom of the bag. You're now ready to sew the sides of the bag closed.

**Step 30** Keep the garment folded up, away from the pocket bag, and now fold it over at the right end of the pocket (see step 19, page 67). With the zipper foot, start sewing the bag closed, stitching close to the end of the pocket opening. Make the first several stitches perpendicular to the opening end, then pivot and continue around the bag, as shown in the photo.

**Step 31** Trim the edges of the pocket bag with pinking shears, or finish with a serger. The pocket is done!

**CHECK THE DEPTH** *tip*
After it's pinned in step 26, the pocket bag should be 1" (2.5 cm) deeper then desired. Shorten it now if you wish.

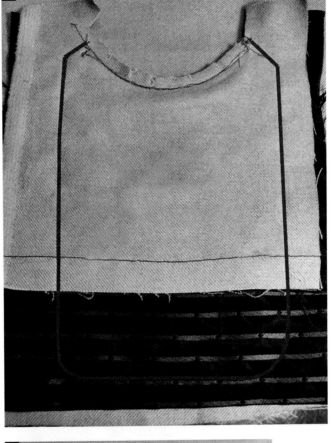

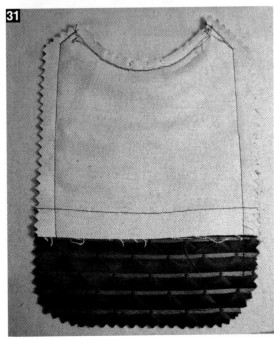

# CHAPTER 5

# *Pockets and* BUTTONHOLES

When you want to create a garment that makes a statement, the pockets and buttonholes serve as the "punctuation." When using punctuation in garment construction as well as in grammar, you want to be precise. Precision in executing the pockets and buttonholes will make a clear statement of your vision for the piece and bear witness to your expertise. In the pockets and buttonholes explained in this chapter, I use some nontraditional materials, such as rattail cord and woven-edge ribbon, to give structure to the work. When used this way for construction, these materials that are more often used for embellishment give reliable, repeatable results.

➋ This lavishly embellished evening dinner jacket sports several classic single welt pockets on the outside and a hidden lining pocket inside. The pockets provide practicality and luxury, too.

# Hidden Lining Pocket

Having a pocket inside a jacket is essential; at least I believe it is. Here's a way to sew a pocket into the seam between the lining and the facing that is not only functional but also attractive. For those who worry about pickpockets, be reassured that this pocket is both invisible and difficult to pick. And since my hidden pocket takes the place of the traditional horizontal inside pocket that goes across the seam between the lining and the facing, it's easy to reline the jacket if you need to in the future. Put your label (if you have one) into the pocket. It's much more tasteful than displaying the label on the back of the neck.

I like to use piping in the seam that joins the lining and the facing. It looks cool and hides the pocket opening, too. Because this pocket hangs to one side of a vertical seam, the edge of the pocket bag opposite the opening tends to fall downward, but I'll show you how to prevent that by sewing a pocket stay—a small strip of fabric—between the pocket edge and the jacket side front seam. Before beginning, review positions 1 and 2 for the adjustable zipper foot (see page 45); you'll use position 1 to make piping and position 2 for other steps.

**Step 1** To draft this pocket onto an existing garment pattern, overlap and pin the front facing and front lining pieces along their shared seamline. Mark the place where you'd like the pocket opening to be (A and B on the drawing at right, referring to the measurements for pocket-opening length on page 46; draw "notches" across the seamline to mark the opening on both pieces. Draw the pocket shape on the lining front as shown. Only seamlines are shown in this drawing; you'll add seam allowances where needed later.

⤴ **A hidden lining pocket sits between the garment lining and facing.**

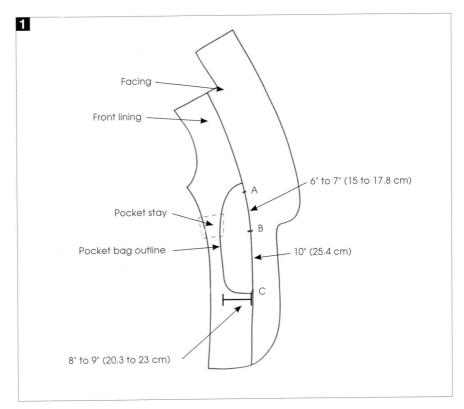

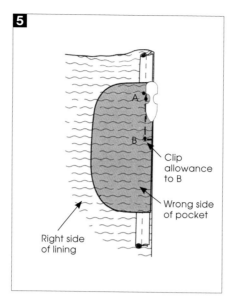

**5**

Clip allowance to B

Wrong side of pocket

Right side of lining

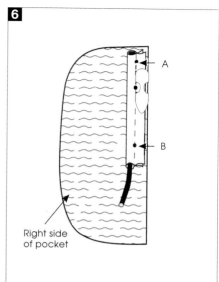

**6**

A

B

Right side of pocket

When placing pockets, es-
pecially on women's jackets,
make sure that the opening is
at or slightly below the bust,
and the depth is enough so that
the contents of the pocket rest
below the bust, not on it.

*tip*

**Step 2** Trace the pocket shape onto another piece of paper, adding the desired
seam allowances. Cut out the jacket,
lining, and pockets from suitable fabrics
and mark all the notches.

**Step 3** Construct the garment and lining
each in its entirety, but don't sew them
together yet.

**Step 4** Measure the total length of the
seamline where the lining will join to the
body. Make a piece of piping 15" (38 cm)
longer than this seamline. Baste the piping to the lining on the seamline; cut off
and reserve the excess. Stitch the piping
in place with the zipper foot in position 2
(this is a final seam).

**Step 5** Pin one pocket piece to the front
edge of the lining, right sides together,
matching the marks. With the zipper
foot in position 2, stitch between points A
and B. Clip at point B.

**Step 6** Cut a piece of piping 1" (2.5 cm)
longer than the distance between the
notches. With right sides together, baste
the piping between the notches on the
remaining pocket piece (the pocket back)
and stitch with the zipper foot in position
2 between points A and B.

**Step 7** Pull the rattail fill completely
out of the piping, and clip as shown at
point B. Press the seam allowances to the
wrong side of the pocket back, as shown
in the drawing.

**7**

A

B

Clip allowance to B

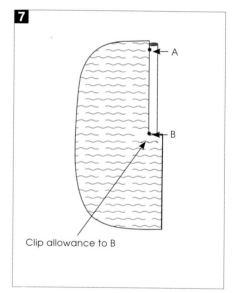

*tip* **NEAT FINISH**
Removing the fill from the piping
reduces bulk when attaching
the pocket back to the facing
and provides an attractive
finish.

**Step 8** Lay the lining piece flat, right side up, with the pocket extended, as shown in the drawing at right. Place the pocket back on top, right side down, aligning the thinned piping right next to the piping stitched to the lining edge, as shown. Pin the pocket pieces together along the outer edge.

**Step 9** Stitch the seam of the pocket only from A to C.

**Step 10** Fold the pocket over along the piping seam onto the right side of the lining. With the zipper foot in position 2, stitch the remaining open side of the pocket to the lining, starting at point B and sewing to the bottom of the pocket, point C.

**Step 11** On the seam just sewn, trim the seam allowances on the pocket to 1/4" (6 mm).

**Step 12** Press all the seam allowances toward the pocket. At the top of the pocket opening (A), stitch with a securing stitch to reinforce that end of the opening. Repeat the procedure at the other end (B). Finish by stitching all the seam allowances onto the pocket from B to C.

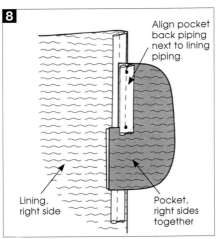

8

Align pocket back piping next to lining piping.

Lining, right side

Pocket, right sides together

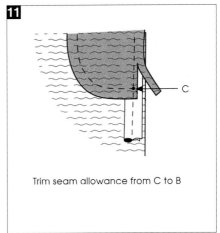

11

C

Trim seam allowance from C to B

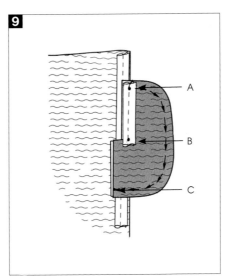

9

A

B

C

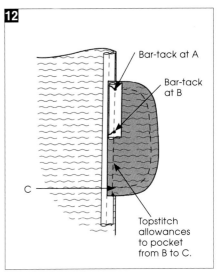

12

Bar-tack at A

Bar-tack at B

C

Topstitch allowances to pocket from B to C.

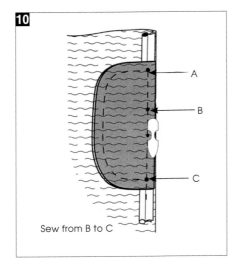

10

A

B

C

Sew from B to C

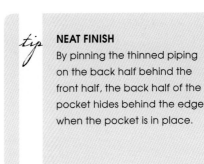

*tip* **NEAT FINISH**
By pinning the thinned piping on the back half behind the front half, the back half of the pocket hides behind the edge when the pocket is in place.

**Step 13** Fold the pocket onto the lining. Create a pocket stay to keep the pocket from curling down into the inside of the garment and inhibiting the free motion of the hand into the pocket. There are two methods. The easiest method is the "tack." If the pocket crosses a seamline, tack the seam allowances of the pocket to the nearest seam allowance.

The second method works best in cases where a seam is further away from the pocket. Sew a strip of organza to the outside seam allowance on the pocket and connect it with the nearest seam allowance on the lining. Organza is best because it keeps its shape while not thickening the piece. Polyester and silk organza are both suitable.

**Step 14** Baste the lining into the garment and try it on yourself or your dress form before continuing. In this way, you'll discover any problems of improper placement before you do the handwork. Attach the lining to the garment with a simple slip stitch. Make each stitch first through the piping flange right between the machine stitches and the fill, and then through the facing, as shown in the photo below. At each end of the pocket opening, reinforce your slip stitch with a few backstitches; be sure to sew only the pocket back to the facing at the opening.

⟳ Here you can see how the running stitch moves between the black velvet jacket facing and the blue lining.

 **HAND-SEWING LININGS**
Divide the lining edge into four or five sections and knot off the thread at the end of each section. Be consistent as to where the breaks occur in every garment. In this way, if you ever need to go back into a garment for repairs or adjustments, you only have to worry about cutting one section, and you'll know exactly where the stitching begins and ends.

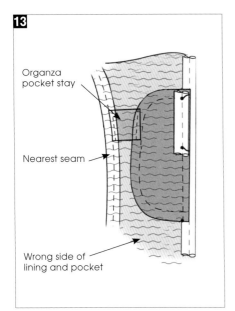

Organza pocket stay

Nearest seam

Wrong side of lining and pocket

⬆ The hidden lining pocket not only has a clean appearance, it also provides security for the pocket contents.

# Hidden Edge Pocket

This is a really nifty pocket; it's a variation of the hidden lining pocket on page 82. The opening is on the edge of the garment, which is completely rimmed by piping, and the pocket doesn't show at all. I use it often for evening wraps when the design doesn't call for a visible pocket, but there's a need for a place to put a compact and lipstick.

Before you can install this pocket, the garment and lining must each be constructed in its entirety and piping must be sewn to the perimeter of the fashion fabric layer. Before beginning, review positions 1 and 2 for the adjustable zipper foot (see page 45). Draft the pocket as explained in step 1 (at right) before cutting out the garment. Make enough piping to rim the perimeter of the garment.

**Step 1** Draft this pocket as you would the hidden lining pocket (see page 79), but position it on the seamline at the edge of the garment (below the bust, ladies!). Mark an opening at least 6" (15 cm) long on the seamline and draw the pocket shape, as shown in the drawing below. At the pocket opening, draft a U-shaped line in the seam allowance as shown; this is the stitching line for the pocket front and lining. Then trace the pocket shape onto another piece of paper; be sure to transfer the straight seamline from your pattern and the U-shaped line you just drew, and add a seam allowance around the rest of the shape if you didn't already do so.

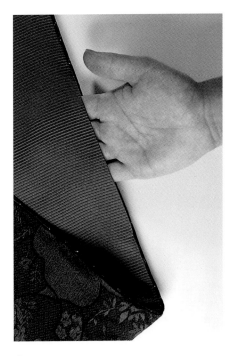

↻ A pocket slipped between the layers at the perimeter is perfect for a garment with a clean design that you don't want to interrupt with a patch or surface opening. The green fabric in this photo is the lining fabric, and the blue fabric is the body of the piece.

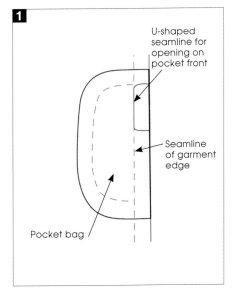

**1**

U-shaped seamline for opening on pocket front

Seamline of garment edge

Pocket bag

**Step 2** Cut out the garment from your fashion fabric. Cut out the lining. Cut two pocket pieces from a suitable fabric. Mark the ends of the pocket opening on the seamline of the garment body (fashion fabric) and one pocket piece, which will be the pocket back. Mark the U-shaped seamline on the lining and the other pocket piece, which will be the pocket front.

**Step 3** Construct the garment and lining each in its entirety, but don't sew them together yet. Stitch the piping to the fashion fabric layer with the foot in position 1. Stitch the pocket front to the lining along the U-shaped line. Use short stitches and place a strip of silk organza cut on the lengthwise grain under the seam for stability.

**Step 4** Grade the seam and clip the inside curves.

**Step 5** Fold the pocket and lining wrong sides together along the seam. Favor the seam toward the pocket piece, and press.

**Step 6** Unfold the pocket front from the lining and pin it, right sides together, to the pocket back; sew them together along the outer edge, as shown in the drawing (A to B).

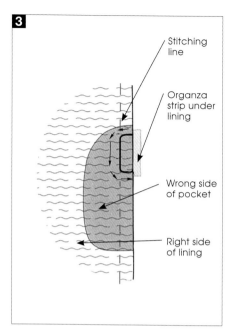

3

Stitching line

Organza strip under lining

Wrong side of pocket

Right side of lining

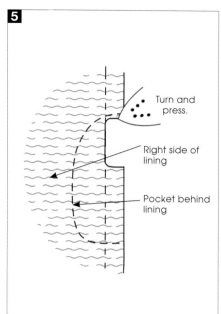

5

Turn and press.

Right side of lining

Pocket behind lining

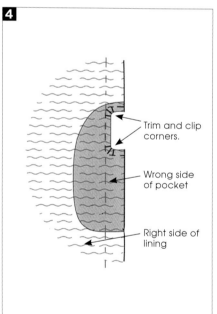

4

Trim and clip corners.

Wrong side of pocket

Right side of lining

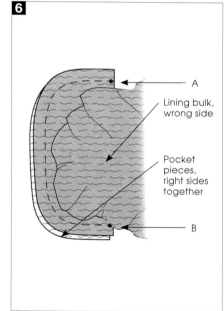

6

A

Lining bulk, wrong side

Pocket pieces, right sides together

B

**Step 7** Fold the pocket back into position against the wrong side of the lining and baste in place.

**Step 8** Place the piped garment and the lining right sides together, aligning the sewn edge of the pocket opening right on the piping sewing line on the garment body; pin through all layers. At the opening, the pocket back forms the seam allowance that will attach to the garment body.

**Step 9** Sew the lining to the body with the zipper foot in position 2. Leave an opening for turning on the bottom or on any straight edge not near the pocket.

**Step 10** Turn the garment right side out. Sew the turning opening closed with a simple running stitch. Press the entire garment perimeter gently so as not to crush the piping; the pocket will seem to disappear.

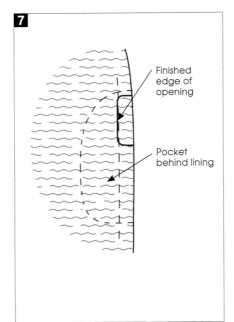

Finished edge of opening

Pocket behind lining

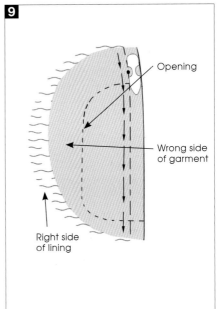

Opening

Wrong side of garment

Right side of lining

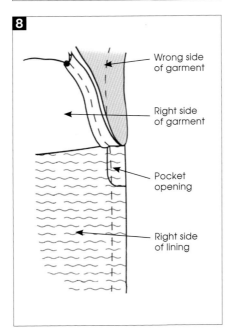

Wrong side of garment

Right side of garment

Pocket opening

Right side of lining

# ℒined Patch Pocket

This blind-hem pocket application is especially nice when you want a patch pocket without topstitching. The finished look is very clean and best on tailored clothing. Here's the trick: You cut the lining a little smaller than the pocket so that when they are sewn together and turned right side out, you can favor the fashion fabric by rolling the seam onto the lined side so it doesn't show from the front. Then when you attach the pocket, because the lining is smaller, you can lift the fashion fabric out of the way to blind-stitch the lining to the jacket, and all the stitches will be concealed when the pocket edge is laid flat again. So the lining performs two functions: First, it will serve to finish the outside edges of the pocket evenly, so no awkward pressing back of seam allowances is necessary. Second, it receives the blind-stitches that secure the pocket to the jacket.

Suggested fashion fabrics for this type of pocket application are wool crepe and any tweed, melton, or other suit-weight fabric. Lining fabrics can match the lining of the garment, or you can work with organza if you want a lighter-weight fabric for a pocket that will not receive much use. Use an adjustable zipper foot to attach the pocket. To see how this works and to make sure the stitch setting is right for you, test the technique on a scrap before using it to attach the pocket to your garment. You want the needle to swing as close as possible to the foot without striking it.

↥ Would you believe blind-hem stitches? That's the way to secure a classic lined patch pocket to a jacket.

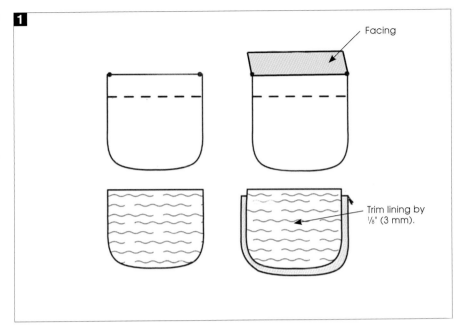

**1**

Facing

Trim lining by
⅛" (3 mm).

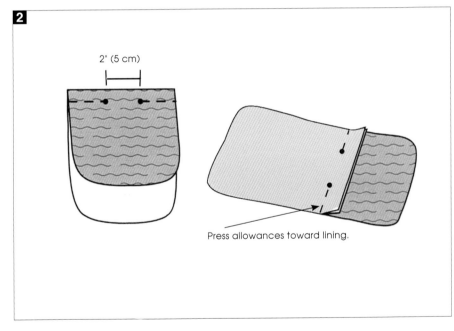

**2**

2" (5 cm)

Press allowances toward lining.

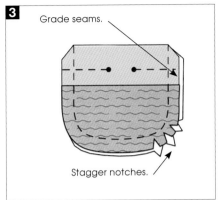

**3**

Grade seams.

Stagger notches.

**Step 1** Draft a paper pattern for the pocket with a 1" (2.5 cm) facing to be folded back at the top edge. Then draft the lining piece to join to the facing, making it ⅛" (3 mm) smaller than the pocket piece on the outside edges. Because the lining is smaller, once you sew the pocket and lining together along the outer edges and turn them right side out, you'll be able to favor the seam by rolling it to the lining side so it doesn't show when the pocket is installed. The illustration shows the pattern seamlines only, so you need to add the desired seam allowances (usually ⅝" [1.5 cm]) before cutting. Cut out the patterns and use them to cut out as many pockets as you need.

**Step 2** With right sides together, sew the lining to the facing edge, leaving an opening of about 2" (5 cm) for turning later. Press the seam allowances toward the lining.

**Step 3** With the right sides together, align the edges of the pocket and lining (taper each facing edge to make a straight line from the lining to the top fold). Pin and sew with lining uppermost, as this will ease the larger pocket onto the smaller lining. Trim the seams and clip the curves.

**Step 4** Turn the pocket right side out through the opening, and press. When pressing, make sure the seam falls to the lining side. Slipstitch the opening closed.

**Step 5** Baste the pocket right side up in place on the right side of the garment piece, placing the stitches about 1/2" (1.3 cm) from the pocket edge. Position the zipper foot far to the right so it sits over one of the rows of feed dog teeth, and move the needle position to the right one notch. Put the work in the machine right side up, ready to sew the right-hand edge of the pocket.

**Step 6** Pull the fashion fabric at the edge of the pocket to the left to expose the seam where the lining is attached, as shown in the photo. The adjustable zipper foot enables you to see exactly where the needle is without impeding the action of the stitch. When starting to stitch, secure your stitches with the securing function on your machine. If your machine doesn't have this function, shorten the stitch length to zero and make a few stitches.

**Step 7** Set the machine for blind hem, as shown below, and begin to sew on the pocket. Stitch all the way around the pocket. At the end, use the securing function to end the stitching, do a final press.

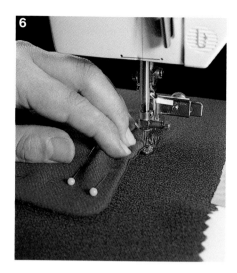

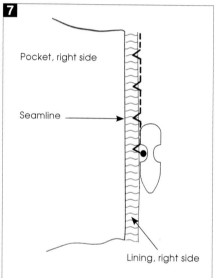

Pocket, right side

Seamline

Lining, right side

 *tip* **BLIND-HEM STITCH**
The zigzag of the blind-hem stitch takes a small bite from the lining fabric. The short stitch length makes the stitch bites closer together for a more secure attachment. Notice that because you stitched to the lining and favored the pocket, all the stitching falls under the pocket piece and is concealed.

**SEWING MACHINE SETTINGS
FOR BLIND HEM STITCH**

**Stitch Width:** *0.6–0.8 mm*
**Stitch Length:** *1.0 mm*
**Presser Foot:** *Adjustable zipper foot*

# $\mathcal{F}$oolproof Single-Welt Pocket

⬆ **The classic single-welt pocket benefits from embellishment.**

With welt pockets, the pocket lining has a tendency to show when the pocket is at rest. This is the kiss of death for the finished look! My welt pocket, constructed with the adjustable zipper foot, is a variation on the industry method of making a welt pocket. This foolproof method relies on a very narrow opening through which to turn the pocket bag, which minimizes the exposure of the pocket interior when the pocket is either at rest or in use.

In commercial patterns, the pocket bag is usually cut in two pieces, but this method is different. The pattern for this pocket bag is one large rectangle, which saves time. The pocket bag can be made from what is called "pocketing twill," but I prefer to use a medium-weight benga-line, moiré, or jacquard. I think a jacket feels more expensive when you put your hand in and feel beautiful fabric. Before you begin, mark the pocket opening on the right side of the garment and review position 1 and position 2 for the zipper foot (see page 45).

**Step 1** To prepare the pattern, decide how deep the welt will be (1" to $1^{1}/_{2}$" [2.5 to 3.8 cm]). The width of the welt must be the size of the pocket opening (see below for the minimum opening sizes). Draw a horizontal rectangle this size on paper, and mark the top edge as the fold line; draw another rectangle the same size on top of the first and then add $^{1}/_{2}$" (1.3 cm) seam allowances all around, as shown. Cut out the pattern; it's ready to use.

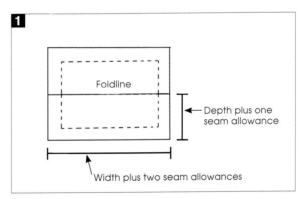

Foldline

Depth plus one seam allowance

Width plus two seam allowances

**Step 2** Cut the welt out of the fashion fabric, laying the welt pattern piece so the foldline (top edge of the pocket welt) is on the crosswise grain. The crosswise grain has more stretch than the lengthwise grain and will help in favoring later. Cut a piece of polyester, silk organza, or any other lightweight woven interfacing fabric to the same size as the welt, with the foldline on the lengthwise grain. The lengthwise grain has the least amount of stretch and will prevent the folded edge from sagging over time.

*tip*

**POCKET OPENINGS**
As a rule of thumb, the best length for a pocket opening is 6" to $6^{1}/_{2}$" (15 to 16.5 cm) for women and 7" to $7^{1}/_{2}$" (17.8 to 19 cm) for men. Pockets can be longer, but these measurements are the minimum for ease of use for most people.

**Step 3** Press the interfacing piece along the foldline and place it on the back side of the welt, lining up the foldline of the interfacing with the foldline of the welt. The area you are placing the interfacing against will be the back of the finished welt, which sits closest to the body, so if you are using a napped fabric, make sure you have the welt oriented correctly. To reinforce the top edge of the welt so it doesn't sag, edgestitch through all layers along the fold of the interfacing. The stitches won't be visible from the front once the welt is folded. For extra reinforcement, stitch a piece of twill tape at the top edge of the interfacing.

**Step 4** With the right sides together, fold the welt in half; turn it so the welt back (the interfaced section) is on the bottom. On each end, favor the welt front by shifting the cut edge by ⅛" (3 mm) at the base of the welt (long edge), tapering to nothing at the top, as shown. Pin and then sew ½" (1.3 cm) from the edge of the welt back.

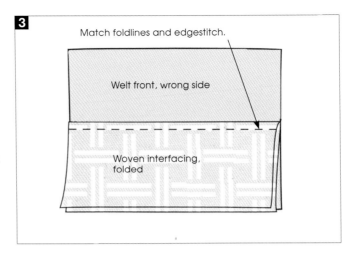

**3** Match foldlines and edgestitch.

Welt front, wrong side

Woven interfacing, folded

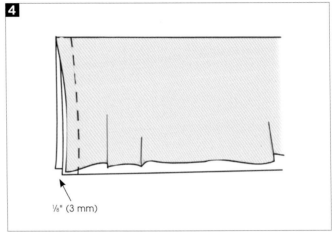

**4**

⅛" (3 mm)

**FAVORING THE SEAMS**

*tip*

Favoring allows you to control where the seams will fall. With the welt pocket, you want the seams to fall toward the back of the welt, so they won't be visible from the front after the welt is stitched into position.

**Step 5** Grade the seam allowances and clip the corners. Turn the welt right side out. Press, stretching the front of the welt to enhance the favoring, and place the seam on the back. Turn the welt so the front faces up, and mark the seamline ¹/₂" (1.3 cm) from the bottom edge.

**Step 6** Draft a paper pattern for the pocket bag. The width must be the width of the welt plus 2" (5 cm). The length is desired pocket depth times 2 plus 2" (5 cm). Cut out the pattern and use it to cut out as many pocket bags as you need.

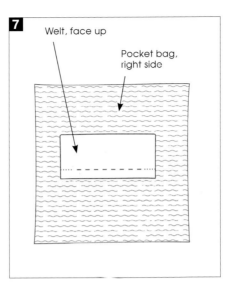

**7**

Welt, face up

Pocket bag, right side

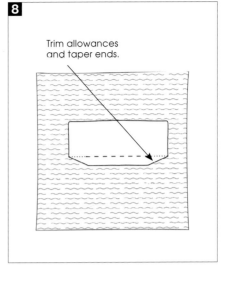

**8**

Trim allowances and taper ends.

**Step 7** With the wrong sides together, fold the pocket bag in half widthwise, and finger-press a crease. Unfold it, lay it right side up, and center the finished welt right side up on it, aligning the chalk-marked seamline over the crease; baste together. Starting exactly at one end of the welt, stitch along the seamline with the zipper foot in position 1 and with the stitch length shortened to 0.5–0.8 mm. Sew with short stitches for ¹/₂" (1.3 cm), then lengthen the stitch to ¹/₈" (3 mm). Stitch the seam until the last ¹/₂" (1.3 cm), then shorten the stitches again. End exactly at the end of the welt.

**Step 8** Trim the seam allowance of the welt to ¹/₄" (6 mm), then taper the ends to almost nothing at the ends of the seam. This narrow seam allowance will help you make the very narrow pocket opening, which will help conceal the pocket bag.

**Step 9** Lay the garment right side up and place the pocket bag right side down on it, with the top edge of the welt pointing toward the bottom of the garment. (If you want to add interfacing to the wrong side of the pocket opening, attach that first.) Align the stitching on the pocket bag with the marked pocket opening on the garment. Baste in place along the stitching line, making an extra tack at each end to secure.

**POCKET DEPTH**

The depth of the pocket should be at least the length of your hand for lower jacket pockets and trouser pockets. For the chest pockets on jackets, my preference is to make them deep enough so a pair of very cool (and expensive) sunglasses won't fall out if you lean forward.

**Steps 10–13** To sew the welt/pocket bag unit to the garment, place the zipper foot to the right of the needle in Position 2 and follow the stitching sequence shown in drawings 10–13. Sew from A to B, shortening the stitches to 0.5 mm length about ½" (1.3 cm) before reaching point B. Pivot 90 degrees at point B, and walk the needle through three stitches. Then, pivot the work again and sew to point C. Continue ½" (1.3 cm) past point C, and then lengthen the stitches again. Sew to point D.

**Steps 14–15** Raise the needle at point D, shift the foot to the left of the needle, and move the foot and the needle to point A (drawing 14). Now repeat the process just completed in reverse, sewing from A to E to F to D, adjusting the stitch length as before (drawing 15).

**Step 16** At this point, check your work before cutting. If, despite your best efforts, you get a gap at the corner of the welt (it does happen—don't panic!), simply turn the entire assembly over and go over the corners again, making sure the zipper foot is snug against the welt. Your new stitching line should be closer in toward the welt than your first stitching line; this will eliminate the gap.

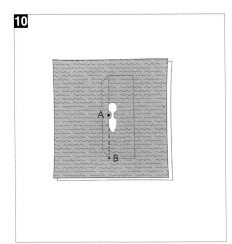

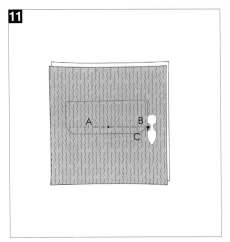

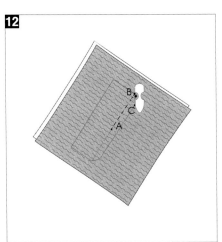

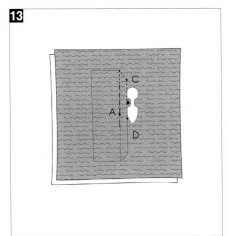

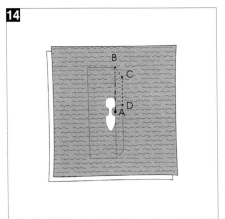

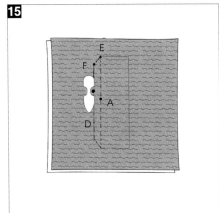

**Step 17** After you've completed and checked your stitching, cut the opening. Start in the middle and cut toward each end, slashing the pocket layer first, then the garment layer. Cut "triangles" at the ends of the opening through all layers, after you cut the two layers, pulling the opening apart slightly.

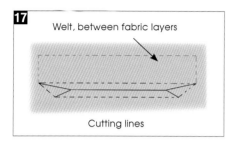

**17** Welt, between fabric layers

Cutting lines

**Step 18** Insert the pocket bag through the opening. From the wrong side of the work, fold down the top of the pocket bag along the seam; finger-press the upper seam allowances and the welt seam allowances downward; press the triangles toward the sides. Turn the work right side up; with the iron, steam and press the welt seam allowances downward.

### SCISSORS STRENGTH

*tip*

Use your sharp tailor's scissors for this because the thick spines at the back of the blades keep the points from separating horizontally when cutting thick fabrics. Weaker scissors won't do the job here.

### AVOIDING END GAPS

By sewing from the center of the welt toward each end, you won't have to jump up onto the welt at the corners; instead, you'll drop off at the ends. Shortening the stitches at the ends keeps the corners from bursting after clipping. Angling in at the corners causes the seamline to fall behind the welt and become invisible.

As you approach the corners, walk the machine one stitch at a time. Stop at the end of the welt! The needle will sound (and, if you are hand-turning the flywheel, feel) different when it has reached the end and is stitching only the fashion fabric and pocket bag. Stop when you hear (or feel) the first stitch that is different.

If in doubt, pull up the pocket piece and look to see if the needle is at the end of the welt. If you go past the end of the welt, there will be a little gap at the end. Most unattractive! Use your point turner to hold the sides of the welt down against the bed of the machine as you are walking up to them. This is especially important at points B and E. Otherwise, the additional thickness makes the fabric want to roll, and slip out from under the foot, causing the seam to be slightly away from where you want it.

The thing to remember here is that it is better to stop short than to go too long. If you stop short, you can fix it, but going too long makes a gap.

**Step 19** Fold the garment piece up at one end of the welt; make sure both layers of the pocket bag lie smoothly toward the side. Repeat at the other end.

**Step 20** Keep the garment folded up at the ends of the welt and now fold the bottom up, too, to reveal the pocket bag. Smooth the layers and pin them together at the edges (don't worry if they don't align exactly). Stitch around the piece with the zipper foot, keeping the seam close to the ends of the welt and sewing through the triangle from the opening on each side; round the corners to prevent lint from gathering in them later. Trim the edges of the pocket bag with pinking shears, or finish with a serger.

**Step 21** Attach the welt ends to the garment by hand-stitching from the wrong side of the garment. Start at the base of the welt and catch the seamline of the welt with each stitch. Go to the top of the welt, then reverse the stitching, ending at the point where you began. In this way, no stitching will be visible from the right side of the garment. The drawing shows the stitch pattern as if the garment were transparent.

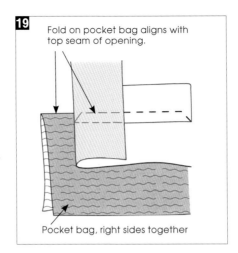

19 Fold on pocket bag aligns with top seam of opening.

Pocket bag, right sides together

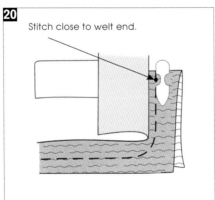

20 Stitch close to welt end.

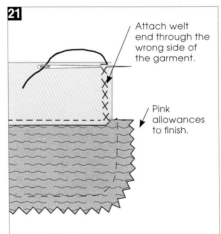

21 Attach welt end through the wrong side of the garment.

Pink allowances to finish.

◔ Welt pockets are used on jackets for the chest pocket and also for lower pockets. You can use them on trousers, too.

◔ Adding decorative embellishment to a single-welt pocket lends unique style.

# $\mathcal{A}$lternate Method for Welts and Flaps

Here's an alternate way to make welts and flaps for pockets. People tell me that my approach to pockets is similar to Judy Barlup's in her excellent work on Japanese tailoring. My method differs most in the handling of the interfacings. The photographed example here is for a pocket flap; just invert the top edge for a welt. If the flap or welt is tapered like the one shown and you need a pair for hip pockets, be sure to cut them so they are mirror images.

The object of the game here, for welts or flaps that have straight edges, is to make sure the edges are all foldlines instead of seamlines. Folded edges make for a really flat, clean welt or pocket flap. To do this, you'll make a pattern that has a facing cut onto each edge; the facings will be shaped to miter on the back of the welt or flap. You need a scrap of organza and a scrap of Hymo for this technique; their size depends on the size of your pattern, as you will see when you read the following steps.

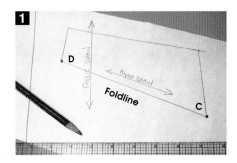

Tape ends closed.

⬆ This flap for a double-welt pocket lies smoothly against the body, and the fabric pattern matches with ease.

**Step 1** So it all starts with the pattern. Draft the desired shape onto the garment front, and then transfer this shape to paper. Make sure you transfer the grainline from the body piece to the welt or flap piece, too. Then mark the top edge of the welt or bottom edge of the flap as a foldline; this line will be the grainline for the interfacings. Fold the paper on this line.

**Step 2** Cut out the pattern along all lines but the foldline. Tape the ends of the pattern closed.

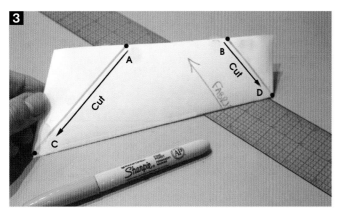

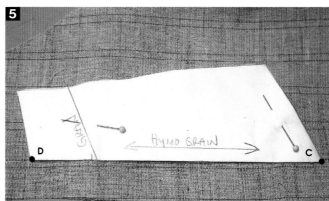

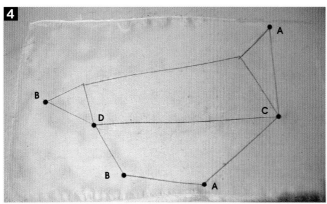

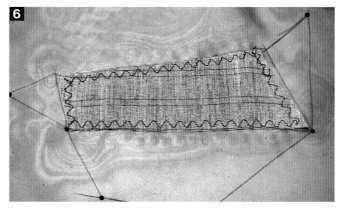

**Step 3** Turn over the pattern. On the back of the pattern, draw two lines (AC and BD), shown here in blue. These are the new seamlines; the exact position of these lines isn't important, they should just be similar to what's shown here. Cut from A to C and from B to D on this layer of the pattern only.

**Step 4** Unfold the paper, and you have your new welt or flap pattern. Transfer the pattern outline and the inner fold-lines onto organza, as shown. Place the foldline (DC) on the straight grain and make sure there is a margin of at least 1" (2.5 cm) all around the pattern.

**Step 5** Fold all the flaps back in place to use the pattern to cut out the Hymo. Place the line DC on the straight grain of the Hymo.

**Step 6** Cut out the Hymo, and then trim ⅛" (3 mm) from each edge. Lay the Hymo on the organza you prepared earlier. In the final piece, the organza will be sandwiched between the Hymo and the fashion fabric. Pin in place. Serpentine-stitch the Hymo to the organza along all edges, using a stitch width of 5.0 mm, stitch length of 1.5 mm.

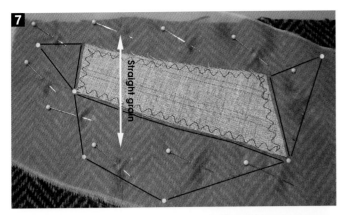

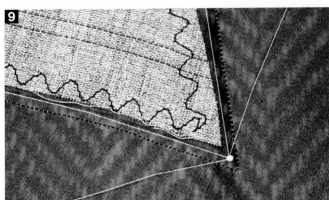

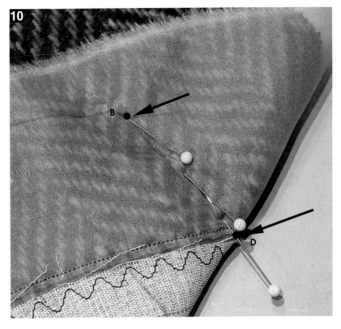

**Step 7** When you are determining the placement of a patterned fabric on the welt or flap, place the organza unit Hymo-side down on the right side of body front, positioning it where it will ultimately be placed. Then you can see the fabric pattern through the organza margin. Draw a grainline and some of the pattern onto the organza margin. Turn over the unit and transfer the markings to the wrong side. (For plain fabric, transfer the grainline from the pattern to the organza.)

**Step 8** To cut the flap or welt, using the marks as a guide, position this unit Hymo-side up on the wrong side of the fashion fabric (so the organza is sandwiched between the Hymo and the fashion fabric). Make sure there is a margin of fashion fabric at least 1" (2.5 cm) all around the outline marked on the organza. Pin. If you like, cut off any excess fashion fabric, leaving the margin.

**Step 9** Sew all the way around the Hymo, stitching $1/8$" (3 mm) outside of the lines drawn on the organza, as shown. An alternative to machine stitching is to sew with a tiny hand-stitch. The hand-stitching makes a join that is almost invisible.

**Step 10** Next, miter the seams on the facing. Match points B and pin along seamline BD. Sew that seam.

**Step 11** Trim the seam and clip the corner.

**Step 12** Now match points A and pin along seamline AC. Sew that seam.

**Step 13** Trim the seam and clip the corner. Working with the point presser, press open the seam allowances.

**Step 14** Turn the welt or flap right side out and press from the back (the faced side). You'll see the mitered seams and the machine stitching parallel to the folded edges.

**Step 15** When you turn the piece right side up, you will see a line of stitching; machine-sew along this line again, through all layers. Then trim the seam allowance at the open edge of the piece to ¹/₂" (1.3 cm).

If you are making a welt, you're done. You can install it following the directions for "Foolproof Single-Welt Pocket," beginning with step 6 (see page 91). To use it for a piped welt pocket, complete step 6 of "Foolproof Single-Welt Pocket," and then continue with step 3 of "Piped Welt Pocket" (see page 100).

## Installing a pocket flap

A pocket flap should be used with a piped welt pocket (see page 100) or a classic double-welt pocket (see page 109). Because the flap conceals the view of the pocket interior, instead of making the pocket bag facing from the fashion fabric, you should make it from the same fabric used for the rest of the bag. It will be less bulky this way. Cut the facing section about 1" (1.3 cm) longer than usual. Use a lightweight interfacing at the top edge, if you like.

**Step 1** Follow the directions for "Piped Welt Pocket" (see page 100) or classic double-welt pocket (see page 109). After inserting the welts and pieces of the pocket bag through the pocket opening (step 11 of completing a piped pocket, page 65), press the seam allowances at the top of the opening up and the ones at the bottom down (so the welts meet in the middle of the opening). Lay the garment right side up and slide the flap into the pocket opening. If you are using a pair of flaps (for a right and a left pocket), make sure you have the correct one in each opening. Align the stitches across the top of the flap with the seam joining the top welt to the jacket. Pin.

**Step 2** Turn the work over. It should look like the photo shown here, with the flap seam allowance extending over the top section of the pocket bag (the facing).

**Step 3** Fold the top pocket bag down, over the cut edge of the flap seam allowance, and pin to the flap only. Fold the body of the jacket away from the enclosed edge and sew the extending, wrapped edge of the flap through all layers, stitching close to the top welting seam as indicated by the arrow.

**Step 4** To finish, follow the directions for steps 13 through 21 of completing a piped pocket (see pages 65–67); these are also the directions for finishing the classic double-welt pocket (page 109).

# $\mathcal{P}$iped Welt Pocket

Sometimes, you may want to make a single-welt pocket with the extra embellishment of piping in the seam at the bottom of the welt. The basic construction method is the same for this pocket as for the "Foolproof Single-Welt Pocket" on pages 84–94, but you'll add the piping to the welt before the welt is sewn to the pocket bag, and so there are a few differences in the process. You'll need a piece of piping the same length as the bottom edge of the welt pattern. Before you begin, mark the pocket opening on the right side of the garment and review position 1 and position 2 for the zipper foot (see page 45); make sure you have an adjustable zipper foot.

**Step 1** Follow steps 1 through 3 of "Foolproof Single-Welt Pocket" on pages 89–90. After the interfacing is stitched to the welt back, baste and stitch the piping to the welt front along the bottom seamline, as shown. Stitch with the zipper foot in position 1 and start and stop $1/2$" (1.3 cm) from each end. At each end of the piping, take out the stitches in the bias cover and hold it open. Then pull the fill gently and cut if off so it doesn't get caught in the seams when you close the welt ends.

**Step 2** Complete steps 4 through 6 of "Foolproof Single-Welt Pocket" on pages 90–91. You don't need to mark the bottom seamline in step 5 because the piping already in place will be your guide later.

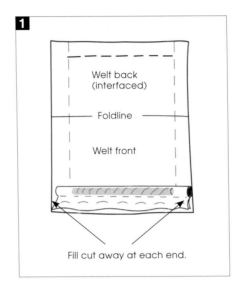

Fill cut away at each end.

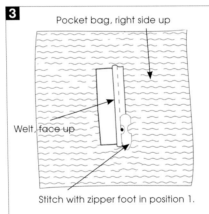

Pocket bag, right side up

Welt, face up

Stitch with zipper foot in position 1.

⬆ **You have several options for pocket treatments. This welt pocket treatment adds a structured finishing touch to classic men's wear.**

**Step 3** With the wrong sides together, fold the pocket bag in half widthwise, and finger-press a crease. Unfold it, lay it right side up, and center the finished welt right side up on it, aligning the piping seamline over the crease; baste

together by hand. Starting exactly at one end of the welt, stitch along the seamline with the zipper foot in position 1 and with the stitch length shortened to 0.5–0.8 mm. Sew with short stitches for $1/2$" (1.3 cm), then lengthen the stitch to $1/8$" (3 mm). Stitch the seam until the last $1/2$" (1.3 cm), then shorten the stitches again. End exactly at the end of the welt.

**Step 4** Trim the seam allowance of the piping and welt to $1/4$" (6 mm), then taper the ends to almost nothing at the ends of the seam. This narrow seam allowance will help you make the very narrow pocket opening, which will help conceal the pocket bag. (See step 8 of "Foolproof Single-Welt Pocket" for a drawing without the piping, page 91.)

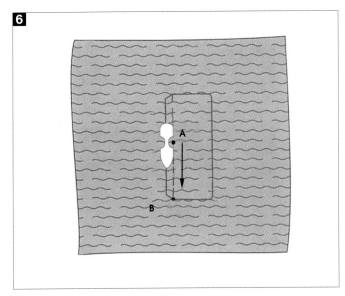

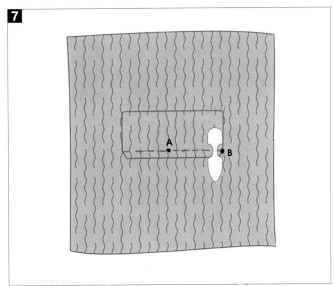

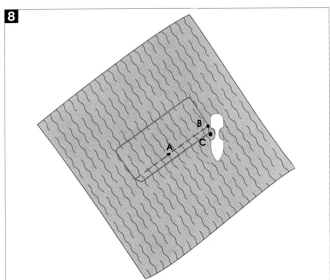

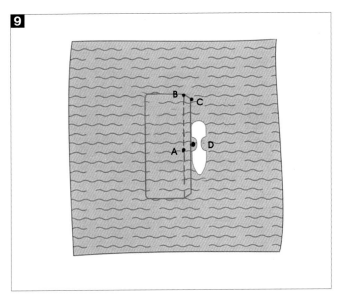

**Step 5** Lay the garment right side up and place the pocket bag right side down on it, with the top edge of the welt pointing toward the bottom of the garment. (If you want to add interfacing to the wrong side of the pocket opening, attach that first.) Align the stitching on the pocket bag with the marked pocket opening on the garment. Baste in place along the stitching line, making an extra tack at each end to secure.

**Steps 6–9** To sew the piped welt/pocket bag unit to the garment, place the zipper foot in position 2 to the left of the needle at point A. Referring to drawings 6–9, sew to point B, shortening the stitches to 0.5 mm length about ¹/₂" (1.3 cm) before reaching point B. Pivot 90 degrees at point B, and walk the needle through three stitches. Then shift the zipper foot to the right of the needle, pivot again, and sew to point C. Continue ¹/₂" (1.3 cm) past point C, and then lengthen the stitches again. Sew to point D.

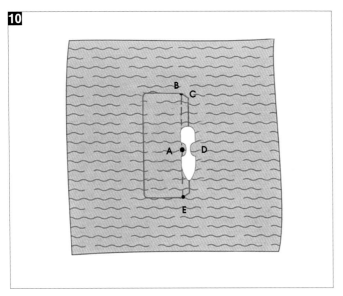

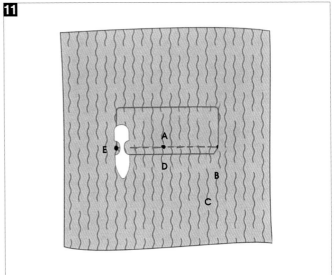

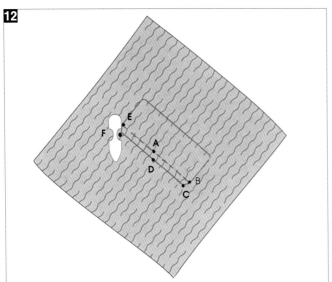

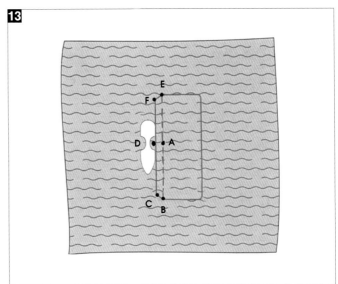

**Steps 10–13** Raise the needle at point D and reposition it at point A, leaving the zipper foot on the right. Now repeat the process, pivoting and adjusting the stitch length as before, but sew from A to E to F to D, shifting the zipper foot to the left when you pivot past point E.

**Step 14** Complete the pocket following steps 16 through 21 of "Foolproof Single-Welt Pocket" on pages 92–94.

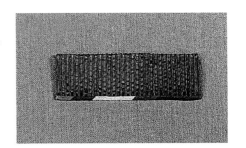

⊙ Piping below a single welt makes a sophisticated pocket finish that can be either sporty or elegant enough for eveningwear.

# $\mathcal{Z}$ippered Ribbon Double-Welt Pocket

This pocket is really useful for clothing and accessories when the security of the pocket's contents is somewhat of an issue—such as expensive sunglasses or that spiffy new cell phone. You'll also see this pocket on outerwear for hiking and other sport activities—those people don't want to lose their cell phones either. I also use it in evening bags and muffs, because it makes a good pocket and looks cool, too. The pocket starts as a long bound buttonhole.

The basis for this pocket is woven-edge ribbon. The size you need (no exceptions!) is ⁷/₈" (2.2 cm) wide; both grosgrain and satin will work. The ribbon interfaces the welts so they stay true and never wobble. At the same time, the ribbon width stands in for a ruler. Instead of measuring the size to cut the welts,

you make them by wrapping the fashion fabric over a length of ribbon and then cutting it in half lengthwise. This welt unit will be 1" (2.5 cm) wide before you cut it in half; after cutting, each welt is ¹/₂" (1.3 cm) wide.

Another thing you need to make a successful zippered welt pocket is a sewing machine foot called a "quilting foot" or "patchwork foot." The outside edges of this foot are each exactly ¹/₄" (6 mm) from the needle. Most sewing machine companies make one of these for their machines, but if your brand doesn't have one, there is a generic foot available. The other foot you'll need is the generic adjustable zipper foot. This is the best foot to sew the ends of the welts with, for finishing.

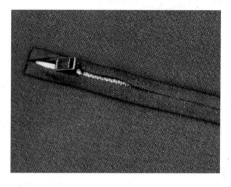

↥ **The zippered welt pocket works really well for sports garb and gear and also for casual clothes.**

You'll also need a zipper. I prefer the metal ones, because they look better under the welts and resist melting when pressed. Get a zipper at least 1¹/₂" (4 cm) longer than the welt opening. A longer zipper will enable you to make a smoother installation; you won't have to dodge around the bulk of the slide at the end.

A piece of fusible interfacing is handy for setting in this pocket. I use fusible tricot for this sample. (I don't generally use fusible for large areas, but it makes setting in this pocket much easier.) Get your fashion fabric and your pocket fabric, and you're ready to go!

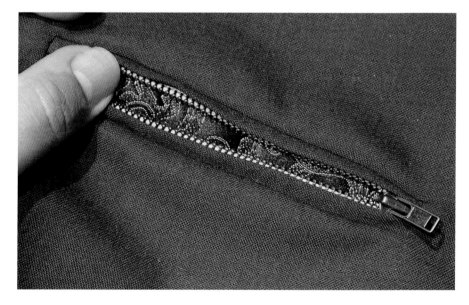

↺ **Choose a jazzy lining for the pocket bag. It'll suprise you every time.**

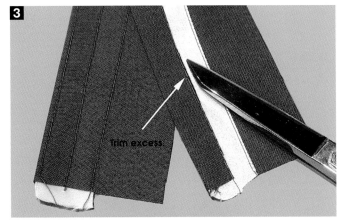

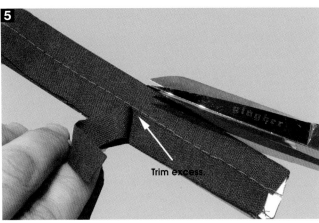

**Step 1** You'll make the welt first. Cut a strip of fashion fabric roughly three times wider than the ribbon and at least 2" (5 cm) longer than the finished opening.

**Step 2** Cut a piece of the ribbon the same length as the fabric strip you just cut. Center the ribbon on the wrong side of the fashion fabric. Machine-stitch ⅛" (3 mm) in from the edge of the ribbon.

**Step 3** Press one side of the fashion fabric over the edge of the ribbon. Machine-baste down the middle of the ribbon strip. Trim the excess fabric close to the machine basting.

**Step 4** Press the opposite edge of the fabric over the opposite edge of the ribbon.

**Step 5** Machine-baste on top of the previous line of machine basting. Trim the excess close to the machine basting.

Note that the front and the back of the finished welt look different; the front has the cut edges of the folded-over fabric; the back has three rows of stitching.

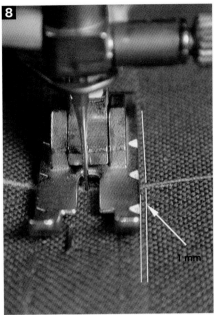

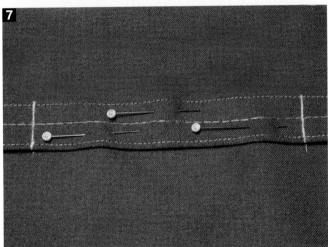

**Step 6** Mark the finished length of the pocket opening on the back of the welt. You are ready to set the welt into the body. Mark the pocket opening onto the right side of the garment with chalk. Interface the wrong side, behind the marked opening.

**Step 7** Place the welt, front down, onto the right side of the garment. If the welt is positioned correctly, you will see three rows of stitching, as in the photo. If you don't see them, turn the welt over. Align the middle row of basting stitches over the pocket opening marked on the garment; align the end marks.

**Step 8** With the quilting foot on the machine, and the welt up, lower the needle onto the end mark, positioning the welt edge so it extends beyond the right edge of the foot by 1 mm, as shown.

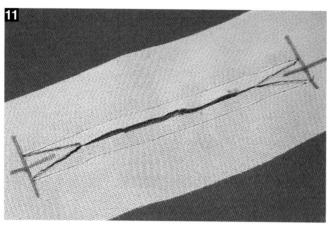

**Step 9** Sew along the edge. Begin with a stitch length of 0.5 mm and continue for about ³/₄" (2 cm). Then lengthen the stitch to 1.5 mm and sew until you get ³/₄" (2 cm) from the end. Shorten the stitch length back to 0.5 mm to finish. Without rotating the work, reposition the foot and needle so the opposite edge of the welt extends beyond the foot by 1 mm and sew in the same way. The welt will torque if you rotate the work to sew the second edge.

**Step 10** Now cut the welt unit only along the row of machine basting in the middle. Don't cut the fashion fabric under the welt yet.

**Step 11** Turn the piece over and, working from the middle toward each end of the opening, cut the fashion fabric, creating triangles at each end, as shown in the photo.

**Step 12** Fold the seam allowance and welt ends to the wrong side through the opening, making sure the ends of the opening are square by laying the piece flat, right side up. Press the opening. At each end of the opening, fold up the fashion fabric, as shown; with the adjustable zipper foot, stitch the triangle onto the end of the welt.

**Step 13** Whipstitch the opening closed with silk thread.

**Step 14** Center the zipper face down on the welt so that the top extends past one end of the pocket opening.

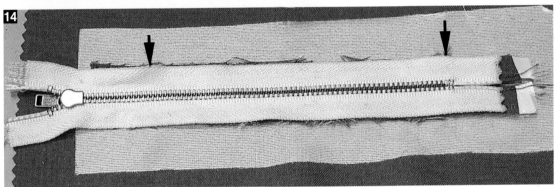

**Step 15** Turn the work over. One side at a time, fold up the fashion fabric and pin the welt seam allowance to the zipper tape, as shown in the photo.

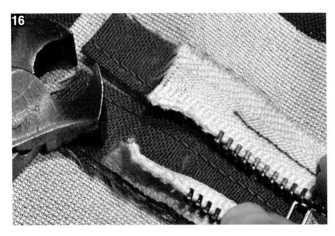

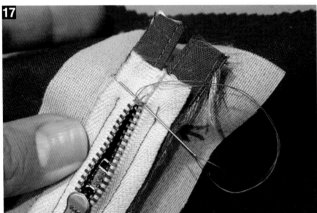

**Step 16** Working with the zipper foot, sew the zipper to each welt as pinned, following the previous stitching. Push the zipper slide down into the pocket opening. With wire cutters, cut away the teeth of the zipper, past the opening, to shorten the zipper.

**Step 17** Hand-stitch the ends of the zipper tape together to make a new "stop."

**Step 18** To make patterns for the pocket bag, follow step 1 of "Completing a Piped Pocket" on page 63. Cut the facing from the fashion fabric and the pocket bag from lining fabric.

**Step 19** Turn the work wrong side up. With right sides together, pin the facing to the seam allowance of the top welt and pin the pocket bag to the seam allowance of the bottom welt. Stitch with the zipper foot, following the previous lines of stitching.

**Step 20** With the work wrong side up, smooth the facing down over the pocket bag and press. To finish the pocket, follow steps 15 through 21 of "Completing a Piped Pocket" on pages 66–68. Remove the stitches holding the welts closed so you can operate the zipper. Now you have your finished zippered welt pocket!

## WELT-BOUND BUTTONHOLE AND CLASSIC DOUBLE-WELT POCKET

Here's a cool thing. You can use this ribbon welt technique to make foolproof welt-bound buttonholes or a classic double-welt pocket without the zipper. Here's what you do.

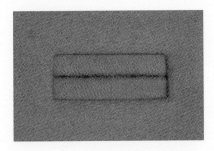

↻ The welt-bound buttonhole works well for tailored clothes that require large buttons.

### Welt-Bound Buttonhole

If you are making a buttonhole in a garment that has heavy interfacing (such as Hymo) under the buttonhole area, make the buttonholes in the fashion fabric layer only. For best results, make them before you attach the interfacing to the project. If you sew a welt-bound buttonhole through the interfacing, it will never press flat.

Follow steps 1 through 10 of "Zippered Ribbon Double-Welt Pocket" (see pages 103–106), substituting the word "buttonhole" for the word "pocket" throughout. Then follow the directions for "Completing a Piped Buttonhole" on pages 59–61, substituting the word "welt" for the word "piping" throughout and ignoring the tip about trimming the fill from the piping.

### Classic Double-Welt Pocket

Follow steps 1 through 10 of "Zippered Ribbon Double-Welt Pocket" (see pages 103–106). Then follow steps 13 through 21 of "Completing a Piped Pocket" on pages 65–67, substituting the word "welt" for the word "piping" throughout.

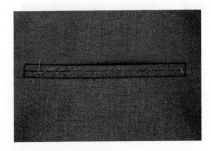

↻ Be sure to baste the two welts together for neat results.

# CHAPTER 6

# The Tailored SHOULDER

Tailoring is the art of creating a garment that imposes an idealized silhouette on the human form. Through tailoring you can strengthen weak shoulders, make an overly thick waist look trim, make a short person appear tall, correct deformities of the body that happened through birth or accident, and otherwise heal all of humanity (well, almost). Through the use of interfacings, padding, stitching, and pressing, you can reshape the form to camouflage what you want, and emphasize the best.

There are two philosophies of tailoring: soft and hard. In hard tailoring, you add support to the shoulder area with extra layers of interfacing called shields. In soft tailoring, you don't.

➲ **This lavish dressing gown of black jacquard and black crushed velvet keeps its shape because of the proper understructure discussed here.**

# $\mathcal{D}$rafting Interfacings

Commercial patterns usually have pattern pieces for the front body interfacing but not the back. The interfacing front is familiar to most, but the half-back (also known as the back stay) is new to some. This piece is cut from cotton batiste or another thin woven fabric. It's put in as a back interfacing piece, which takes strain off the fashion fabric when the garment is worn.

An advantage to the half-back is that it provides a foundation on which to stitch the shoulder pads. Stitching the edges of the shoulder pads to the half-back prevents the pads from curling over time (otherwise, they will!). It also keeps the edges of the pad from reading through to the outside of the garment. If you would like a really built-up shoulder, you can make shields for the back, too, and attach them to the half-back (see page 116). If there are no interfacing patterns, draft them, referring to the drawing in step 1 for the front and step 2 for the back. Add the seam allowance to any edges that don't already have one.

**Step 1** If you are drafting a pattern for the front interfacing, make it about 1" to 2½" (2.5 to 6.5 cm) narrower than the front facing at the bottom edge. Cut the front interfacing from Hymo (hair canvas, see page 14) and a "thin, cheap"

fabric. Assemble these pieces as described in the section Installing Hymo the Easy Way on page 17. Then set the interfacing aside until you have cut out the front shields (see page 117), if you are using them, or until you are ready to assemble the garment.

**Step 2** If you are drafting the half-back interfacing, make it 6" to 8" (15 to 20 cm) deep at the center back and about 3" (7.6 cm) deep below the armscye. Cut the half-back interfacing from cotton batiste. Set it aside until you have cut out the back shields, if using (see page 116), or until you are ready to assemble the garment.

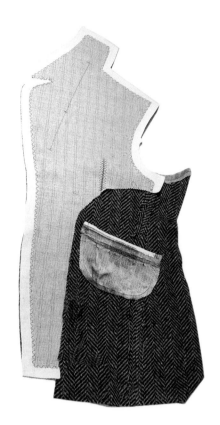

⬆ Here you can see where to interface a jacket front.

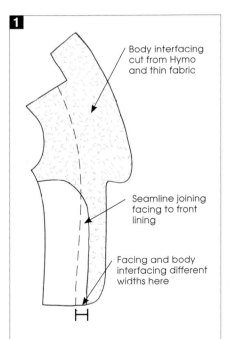

Body interfacing cut from Hymo and thin fabric

Seamline joining facing to front lining

Facing and body interfacing different widths here

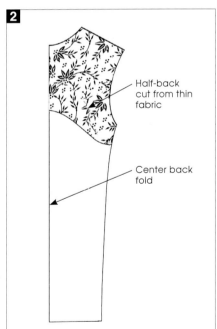

Half-back cut from thin fabric

Center back fold

# $\mathcal{P}$reparing the Sleeve Pattern

For a tailored set-in sleeve, there should be no more than 1" to 1¼" (2.5 to 3 cm) of ease in the cap. The optimum is 1" (2.5 cm). Measure and compare the armhole seamlines of the sleeve pattern and the jacket front and back patterns, and adjust the sleeve pattern, if necessary. If there is too much ease, you have two choices. Either remove the excess by lowering the cap in ⅛" (3 mm) increments until the excess is gone, or slash the pattern from cap to cuff and overlap the cut edges at the cap edge to eliminate the excess.

The slash-and-overlap method works for those patterns with a sleeve cap that is too low to begin with. In general, use the slash-and-overlap method rather than lowering the sleeve cap. After narrowing the cap, use a flexible ruler to outline a smooth curve along the top.

There's a third way to remove the ease, and it should be used if you don't want to lose any of the sleeve volume around the bicep. Instead of slashing and overlapping the pattern or lowering the cap, lower the armhole on the body. Be sure to lower the front and back equally. Walk your tape measure along the armhole seamline to see where to draw the new line. Its length should be 1" to 1¼" (2.5 to 3 cm) less than the length of the sleeve cap seamline.

⊙ With just the right amount of ease, a sleeve sits smoothly in the armhole.

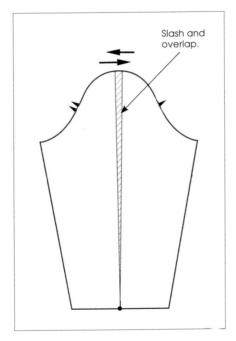

Slash and overlap.

⊙ A tiny waist is accentuated by the proper fit of shoulder and sleeves.

# $\mathcal{E}$asing the Sleeve Cap

After you've cut out and constructed the sleeve, you'll ease the sleeve cap onto a sleeve head. Sleeve heads, for those not familiar with them, are strips of padding that fill in the fold between the seam allowance on the sleeve cap and the sleeve cap itself. This padding gives the sleeve cap a smooth contour where it sets into the armhole. If you omit the sleeve head, you will have little puckers all along the sleeve cap.

The method described here is a variation of the "lamb's wool" sleeve head method described in the book *Power Sewing* by Sandra Betzina. In the technique presented here, you will work with loosely woven wool/mohair blend fabric for the sleeve heads. This fabric is more expensive than lamb's wool, but you can buy ³⁄₈ yard (34.3 cm) and get quite a few sleeve heads from it. Some of my correspondents tell me they have great success using polar fleece as a substitute. A wool and mohair blend is preferable to silky pure mohair, because the silkier fibers find their way to the outside of the piece. With this technique, you will install the sleeve head and ease the sleeve in one operation, which will save time.

↷ A beautifully tailored shoulder, consisting of sleeve heads and shoulder pads as support, produces a crisp line on any tailored jacket.

**Step 1** Cut the strips of mohair on the bias, 3" (7.5 cm) wide and 1½" (4 cm) longer than the sleeve cap length between the notches on the pattern. If you are precutting, a length of 11" (28 cm) will serve all purposes. Place a strip on the wrong side of the sleeve cap, extending one end 1" (2.5 cm) past one notch and lining up one edge with the cut edge of the sleeve. Starting at the notch, and placing the stitches in the seam allowance ⅛" (3 mm) in from the seamline, sew a few stitches by machine.

Continue sewing by machine, stretching the strip as much as possible (like you're hanging off a cliff) while sewing it all along the sleeve cap. Stop stitching at the opposite notch and cut off the excess strip 1" (2.5 cm) beyond the notch.

**Step 2** Shake the sleeve. The ease will automatically fall into place evenly. The mohair will not cave in as readily as cotton sleeve heads will, and the fiber will fluff up with steam. This treatment will eliminate those annoying puckers that often form on sleeve caps.

**Step 3** Install the sleeve into the armhole as usual. Baste before sewing to check the fit. An advantage to basting is that the layers can be held in their final relative positions, so you can run the whole garment through the sewing machine in any direction that is convenient.

After trimming and clipping and so forth, add the shoulder pad in the usual manner. Steam the entire shoulder after the pad is in place, holding it over your hand and letting it hang as it will when worn. When your hand is scorched, you know it's well pressed!

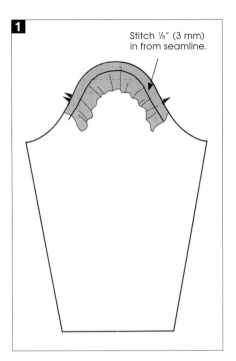

Stitch ⅛" (3 mm) in from seamline.

**ATTACHING THE LINING**

When installing the lining into the garment, before you close up the edge, stitch the seam allowances of the lining armhole to the fashion fabric armhole under the arm between the ends of the shoulder pads. The sleeve lining will be right side out, which allows the seam allowances to fall into the sleeve, keeping them in the same direction as the upper portion of the seam, held by the shoulder pad. This also prevents the lining from roaming around inside of the garment.

⬆ In addition to the proper easing, the success of this particular sleeve is in the matching of the pattern to the body.

# Supporting the Shoulder

The support inside the shoulder area of a tailored jacket keeps the fashion fabric smooth and ensuring that the jacket keeps its nice shape over a part of the body that moves a lot. It keeps the top of the sleeve sleek, too. In addition to the interfacing that covers the entire front area, there are two things that give a garment this needed support: shields and shoulder pads.

Shields you make from hair canvas (Hymo) and sometimes horsehair canvas. I explain three types here: the standard, which will be supplemented with a purchased shoulder pad; a large type to use when you need to level uneven shoulders, also supplemented with purchased shoulder pads; and another type I call a "flat shoulder pad," which has no padding and works where you want just a little extra support but don't want the added height of a shoulder pad.

## Making standard shoulder shields

Shields are small shaped pieces of interfacing applied in layers to stiffen the area between the armhole and the lapel, so the garment won't fall into the dip between the shoulder joint and the chest. You'll cut the shields out of horsehair canvas (see page 14), rotating the orientation of the shoulder seam on the horsehair 90 degrees on alternating layers. The only reason you might want to make back shields would be if you want a really, really wide shoulder, like the ones on zoot suits. In that case, back shields will help support the additional weight.

⬆ The smooth cap and perfect hang of this sleeve are the hallmarks of a well-tailored shoulder.

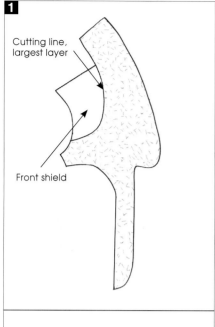

**1**

Cutting line, largest layer

Front shield

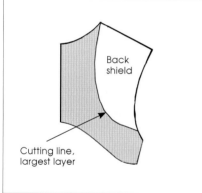

Back shield

Cutting line, largest layer

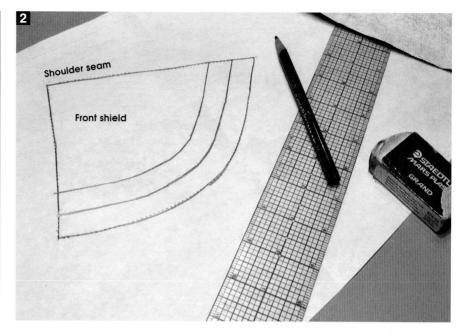

**2**

Shoulder seam

**Front shield**

STAEDTLER
MARS PLAS
GRAND

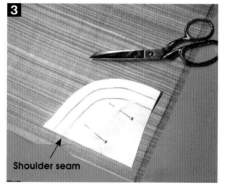

**3**

Shoulder seam

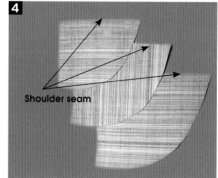

**4**

Shoulder seam

**Step 1** Draft the patterns for the largest layer of the front shield and the back shield, as shown in the drawings. Draft them onto the existing interfacing or half-back pattern, making each about 5" to 7" (12.5 to 18 cm) deep along the armscye edge, depending on whether the armhole is large or small.

**Step 2** Trace each shield pattern onto fresh paper, omitting the shoulder and armhole seam allowance. On each of these, draw two more lines parallel to the bottom edge and about ³⁄₄" (2 cm) apart, as shown in the photo.

**Step 3** For each shield, cut the largest piece with the shoulder seam parallel to the horsehair (on the cross-grain of the canvas).

**Step 4** Cut the second layer with the shoulder seam perpendicular to the horsehair. Cut the smallest layer with the shoulder seam parallel to the horsehair.

 *tip*

**QUICK CUTTING**

If you like, make a separate pattern for each size from the largest shield pattern, or plan to cut two of the largest and then trim off the extra to cut the two middle-sized and then the two smallest pieces.

**Step 5** For each shield, stack the three layers, matching the shoulder and armhole lines. Lay them on the wrong side of the body interfacing (the side that will be closest to the body), aligning them with the cut edges of the Hymo. Pin the pieces to the Hymo.

**Step 6** With a walking foot, stitch the layered pieces to the interfacing, sewing a grid over them with a serpentine stitch, as shown in the photo.

When you turn the piece over, only the machine stitching is visible, so the cut edges of the shield, which are underneath, won't "read through" the fashion fabric.

### SEWING MACHINE SETTINGS FOR SHIELD ATTACHMENT

*Stitch:* Serpentine
*Stitch Width:* 5.0 mm
*Stitch Length:* 2.5 mm

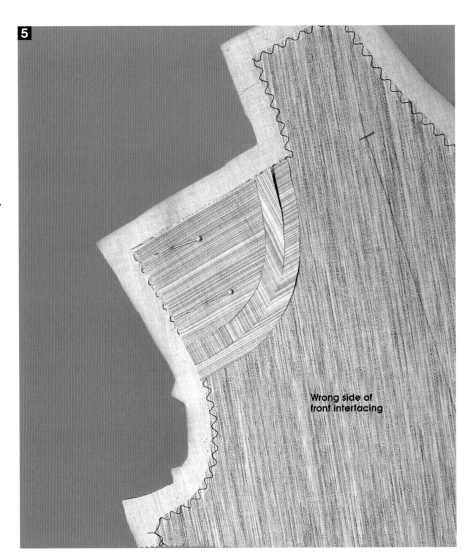

Wrong side of front interfacing

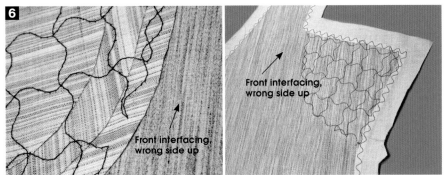

Front interfacing, wrong side up

Front interfacing, wrong side up

## SHOULDER PADS

When making jackets with set-in sleeves, you need a shoulder pad. Thank heaven we got past that period in fashion when men's jackets went without. Everyone just looked frumpy! There are two types of shoulder pads, for set-in sleeves and for raglan sleeves. As you will see when you purchase shoulder pads, there is an astounding variety to choose from. The set-in pads fall into two broad categories: nonwoven (including the foam pads) and stitched. By set-in pads, I'm talking about the kind you buy at tailoring suppliers, those that will live inside a lining. We are not covering raglan sleeve pads, or the taffeta-covered foam rubber pads used in blouses or dresses.

**Nonwoven pads** are usually covered with a pellon or synthetic felt fabric. The filling—foam or synthetic fibers, and sometimes cotton—is fused to the pad. The padding looks like layers of synthetic felt fused together by heated needles (called needle-punch pads). I would caution you against the use of foam rubber pads, because they dry out and crumble over time, and they make a real mess inside the garment when they start crumbling. They are also prone to decomposition when dry-cleaned.

**Stitched pads** are covered with either pellon or woven cloth and are filled with batting (as opposed to layers of felt), which is stitched together by hand or machine with big stitches. These pads tend to be softer and need to be pressed over a ham before they are installed.

Some pads have really stiff coverings, just the thing to have when making shoulders that will clear off shelves in department stores as you walk by! These pads can be different thicknesses, but my favorite is about ½" (1.3 cm) thick with a compact cotton fill fused to the pad. They tend to be firm, and to increase the thickness you can stack more than one.

The advantage of a stitched pad is that you can take it apart to add or remove filling to customize the pad. If you are filling out a shoulder pad, use cotton batting and press it into layers before adding it to the pad. When you have the desired thickness, stitch the pad together with big stitches that are secure but not tight.

Start in the center of the pad and work outward in rows, shaping the pad over your hand as you go. If you build in the shape while sewing, the pad will hold its shape for the life of the garment. Always press the pad over a ham before installing.

You should purchase your shoulder pads early in the project, because you'll want to fit your muslins with the intended shoulder pads. Yes, you should make a muslin sample garment! Otherwise, you will have an unpleasant surprise when you make up your garment in fashion fabric. The shoulder pad is installed after the sleeve is set in, but before you sew in the lining.

This casual fringed jacket benefits from the structure provided by properly tailored shoulders. The structure not only improves the appearance and form, but also makes the jacket more durable.

120

## Making a flat shoulder pad

Occasionally, you may wish to make a tailored coat with no added height at the shoulder. In this case, you need a pad that supports the shoulder with no padding. To make this type of pad, you use layers of interfacing fabrics.

**Step 1** For the pattern, use any tailored shoulder pad to get the outline and the line that matches the garment shoulder. If you don't have a shoulder pad, align your front and back jacket patterns at the shoulders and draw a shape like the one shown. Draw two lines (B and C) 3/4" (2 cm) away from one another, parallel to the outline (A), as shown. Trace three shoulder pad patterns on fresh paper, one following each outline. Cut layer A on the bias from Hymo canvas. Cut layers B and C from hair canvas with the horsehair oriented as indicated by the arrows on the drawing.

**Step 2** Stack the pad layers in sequence, aligning the armhole edges. If you installed this pad as you would a traditional pad, it would ripple, so you need a different method. Machine-stitch the layers together with parallel rows of stitching 1/2" (1.3 cm) apart. Align a piece of 1/2" (1.3 cm)-wide horsehair braid on the armhole edge on the Hymo side of the pad; sew it to the pad with two or three rows of straight stitching. The horsehair braid keeps the edge true after assembly —otherwise, the weight of the sleeve cap could cause the sleeve to ripple.

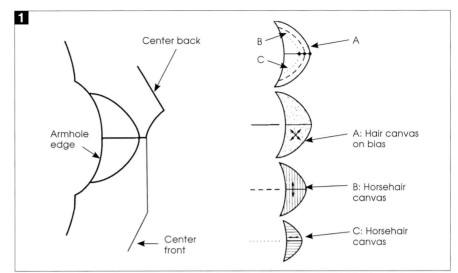

Center back

Armhole edge

Center front

B
C
A

A: Hair canvas on bias

B: Horsehair canvas

C: Horsehair canvas

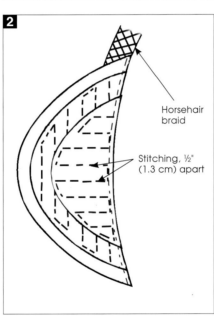

Horsehair braid

Stitching, 1/2" (1.3 cm) apart

**Step 3** When appropriate for the garment you're making, set the sleeves into the armholes. Do any clipping that your pattern requires. Then place the jacket on the dress form. Place the pad, with the Hymo side up, in the jacket. The edge of the pad will extend, at most, 1/2" (1.3 cm) into the sleeve cap. After pinning the pad to the garment, while the garment is still on the form, hand-baste the pad securely in place through all layers along the armhole seamline and outer edge. Once basted, the shoulder pad can be stitched into place by hand. First, stitch the armhole edge to the sleeve-cap seam allowances. Then tack the outer edge to the jacket interfacing.

## Leveling uneven shoulders

Occasionally, a person may have one shoulder that is significantly lower than the other. In a tailored garment, you want a level shoulder line—so a significant difference in shoulder height really shows up.

I define "significant difference" as a case when one or more complete shoulder pads needs to be added to raise the level of the low shoulder to match the higher one. I've had cases where I've added two extra pads, to make a total of three pads on one side and only one on the other. When you have this sort of significant difference, you need to reinforce the entire shoulder area by making a larger than normal shoulder shield from hair canvas. You shape this shield like an oversized shoulder pad and then pad it to compensate for the difference in height. In fact, you can think of this shield as a combination pad and shield. When you use it, you should omit the standard shield from the garment.

This large shield covers both the front and the back and extends to the neckline. The shield needs to go all the way to the neck. Otherwise, when you stack up the pads, the shoulder line will cave in about 2" (5 cm) from the neck. You should install a large shield on both shoulders for balance. If you used one only on one shoulder, the garment would feel odd to the wearer. Be careful when

you make these, because you need a pair—one for the right shoulder and one for the left. Be sure to turn the pieces over when necessary so you don't make two alike.

After the canvas shields are installed in the garment, you will add a different amount of padding underneath each, to level out the shoulders. I like the needle-punch pads for this operation, because the layers of "felt" are easier to stack up to modulate the different thicknesses for the different shoulder heights. Buy several sizes so they can taper in width when you layer them in the garment.

**Step 1** Prepare the shield patterns. Align your jacket front and back patterns at the shoulders and draw a shape like the one shown. Draw two lines (B and C) $^{3}/_{4}$" (2 cm) away from one another, parallel to the outline (A), as shown. Trace three shoulder pad patterns on fresh paper, one following each outline. Mark the shoulder seamline on each one. Cut the layers out of horsehair canvas, aligning the shoulder seamline perpendicular to the horsehair (cross-grain) on the largest and smallest layers, and parallel to the horsehair on the middle layer. Mark the shoulder seamline on each piece and indicate which portion is the garment front.

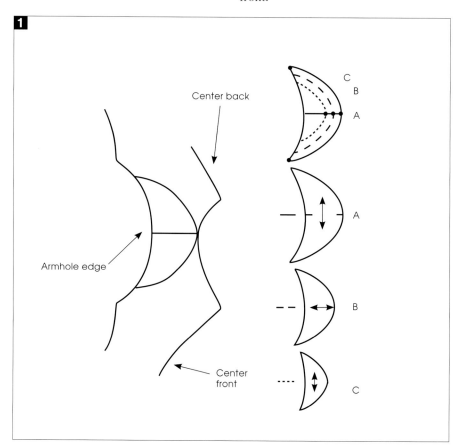

**Step 2** Stack the shield layers in decreasing sequence, aligning the armhole edges and shoulder seamlines. Make sure you have a pair, with the garment front sections on opposite ends. Machine-stitch the layers together in a large zigzag pattern, going back and forth between the armhole and the outer edge. Then, turn the shield so the underside faces up (with the smallest layer on top) and with a serpentine stitch, sew a strip of ¹/₂" (1.3 cm)-wide horsehair braid along the armhole edge.

**Step 3** Cut a 1¹/₂" (3.8 cm)-wide bias strip of muslin. Press it to shape it into a curve that matches the armhole edge of the shield. Cut the strip to the length of the armhole edge of the shield.

**Step 4** Turn the shield so the upper side (largest layer) faces up. Overlap the muslin strip on the armhole edge. Sew it on with a serpentine stitch.

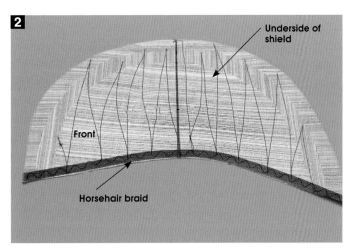

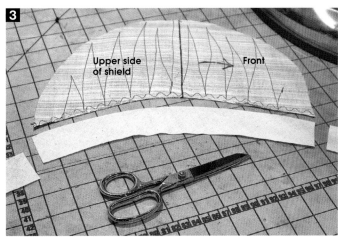

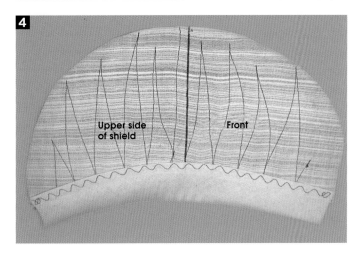

**Step 5** The shields are ready to install in the jacket; put them in whenever your pattern instructions say to add the shoulder pads. Place the upper side of the shield against the wrong side of the jacket; make sure the front of the shield is oriented to the front of the jacket. Match the shoulder line to the shoulder seam, placing the cut edge of the shield on the armhole seamline (shown with the muslin folded over the edge in this photo in order to show the seamlines).

**Step 6** Pin the muslin strip to the armhole seam allowance, lining up the cut edge of the shield with the seamline.

**Step 7** Sew the muslin to the seam allowance with a loose running stitch. Make this line of stitching about 1/8" (3 mm) from the seamline. (Use matching thread; the contrast in the photo is for clarity.)

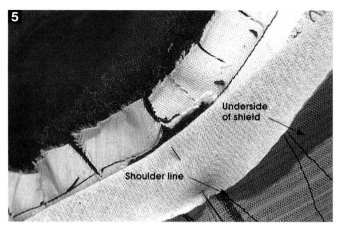

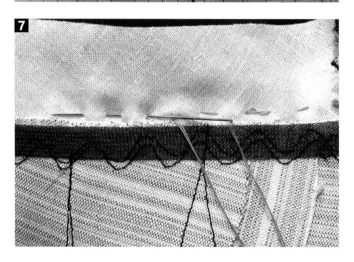

**Step 8** Fold back the front facing and tack the free edge of the shield to the jacket shoulder seam. Leave the rest of the edge unattached.

**Step 9** Stack the shoulder pads needed to raise the lower shoulder, arranging them so the largest layer is on top, the smallest on the bottom, and loosely stitch them together. Place the pad in the jacket, putting the top of the pad against the shield and aligning its armhole edge with the cut edge of the jacket armhole; pin along the seam allowance.

**Step 10** Pin the pads so the edge of the pad lines up with the cut edge of the seam allowance of the armhole. Stitch the pad to the seam allowance with a loose running stitch, sewing through all the layers about $\frac{1}{8}$" (3 mm) from the seamline.

**Step 11** Now tack the pad to the shield, using a catchstitch, as shown, so the pad won't curl over time.

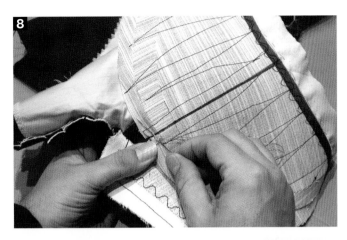

# Preparing Lining Patterns

Make the entire lining before installing it into the jacket. Some modifications are necessary. You need to accommodate for the mass of the shoulder pad by lowering the shoulders and dropping the sleeve cap. Also, you want the lining slightly shorter than the garment—about ¾" (18 mm)—so you don't have the hem of the lining peeking out from under the hem of the garment. As for body circumferences, I know there are debates raging. There are some who say to cut the lining smaller than the body, some say larger. I cut them the same. It works for me.

**Step 1** Check the sleeve cap height of the lining in relation to the fashion fabric sleeve (points A to B). It should be about ½" (1.3 cm) lower to accommodate the shoulder pad.

**Step 2** On the body of the jacket, lower the shoulder line (points A to B) at the armhole slightly, ¼" (6 mm) front and back, to compensate for the pad. This adjustment will keep the lining from bunching at the shoulder.

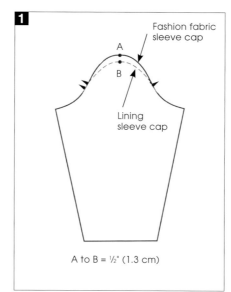

**1**

Fashion fabric sleeve cap

A

B

Lining sleeve cap

A to B = ½" (1.3 cm)

A luxurious lining makes the inside of a jacket just as special as the outside. To finish the effect, the lining is joined to the facing with piping.

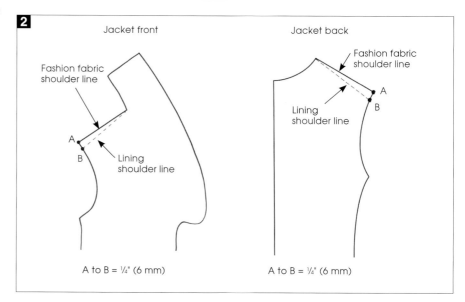

**2**

Jacket front

Fashion fabric shoulder line

A

B

Lining shoulder line

A to B = ¼" (6 mm)

Jacket back

Fashion fabric shoulder line

A

B

Lining shoulder line

A to B = ¼" (6 mm)

A slippery lining adds comfort and makes the garment easy to put on and take off. A fabulous lining fabric adds luxury, too.

# CHAPTER 7

# DESIGNER
## *Embellishments*

Embellishments are the icing on the cake, so to speak. They provide an opportunity to personalize your work and let your garments show the world who you are. When using embellishment, however, I have one caution: Don't make the piece a showcase for embellishments, but use the embellishments judiciously to enhance the piece. When in doubt (I can't believe I'm writing this!), less is more. Knowing when to stop is just as important as knowing how to press a seam well. (When people look at my garments, they ask me how I know when to stop. I just do, I can't explain it.) So, with this, I send you forth to explore the wonderful world of embellishments. Enjoy them as much as I do!

➲ In sewing, as in beauty, you need the right finishing touches. For beauty, it can be just the right color of foundation or lipstick, but for sewing, you need something a little more substantial.

# Pleated Ruffle

This pleated ruffle has a stiffened edge, so it really flutes dramatically. It is easy to make and looks like a million bucks. Start with fabric that is already pleated, either with a tiny knife pleat, crystal pleat, or mushroom pleat (see "Glossary," page 170). Stiffer fabrics work better for this technique—taffeta, for example—but other fabrics are also appropriate. Prepleating creates a sort of "boning" effect that stiffens limp fabric to keep the ruffles erect. But if you don't have pre-pleated fabric, you can use this technique to stiffen the edge of flat fabric and then gather the other edge to ruffle it.

To determine the cut width of the fabric, first decide how far you want the ruffle to extend from the seam; to this add $^{1}/_{2}$" to $^{5}/_{8}$" (1.3 to 1.5 cm) for seam allowance so you can sew it on plus $^{1}/_{2}$" (1.3 cm) for finishing the loose edge. To determine the length of the strip for prepleated fabric, measure the seamline to which you're attaching the ruffle and add one-third this amount. For example, if the seam is 12" (30.5 cm), the strip will measure 16" (40.5 cm) long. You want extra fabric in the seam so the edge will create more "sweep." For flat fabric, cut the strip three times the length of the seamline, following the "three times" rule at right, sew strips together to make one long strip, if appropriate.

A sheer pleated ruffle is full of nuance and drama.

**THE "THREE TIMES" RULE**
Length times three is the best way to figure the amount of fabric needed for gathering, whether you're making curtains, skirts, or an edging. Two times is skimpy, and two and a half is harder to multiply. "Three times" is an old theater trick. You can get away with using cheap fabric if you have more length when gathering.

## Stiffening the edge

There are two ways of finishing the edge and both use monofilament thread—you know, fishing line! A good weight for this purpose is 20-lb. (9 kg) test, big game line, bought at sporting goods stores. Bring your own spool, because this stuff is sold in bulk and is wound directly onto the fishing reel. The first way to finish the edge is the easiest: Use a serger set to a 3-thread rolled hem and fitted with a cording foot, inserting the monofilament as you go. This method is quick, tidy, and efficient. For those of you who don't own a serger, you can just use your sewing machine fitted with a pintuck foot, setting it to the zigzag stitch as indicated in the box at right. It's a little more time-consuming but worth the effort; here's what you do.

### SEWING MACHINE SETTINGS

*Stitch:* Zigzag
*Stitch Width:* 0.6–0.8 mm
*Stitch Length:* 4.0–5.0 mm

**Step 1** Lay the prepleated strip wrong side up on your ironing board. Pull the fabric flat and fold up and press a "bend" ½" (1.3 cm) from the raw edge along the edge to be finished.

**Step 2** Place the strip wrong side up under the sewing machine presser foot, with the crease of the "bend" centered on the throat plate. Zigzag the monofilament into the crease, which forms a valley that the monofilament falls into.

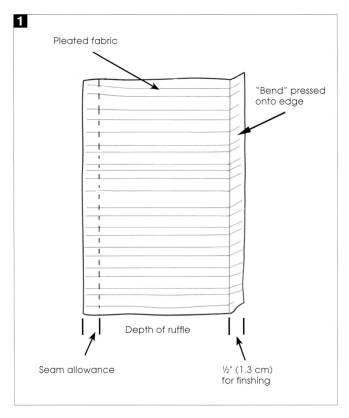

Pleated fabric

"Bend" pressed onto edge

Depth of ruffle

Seam allowance

½" (1.3 cm) for finshing

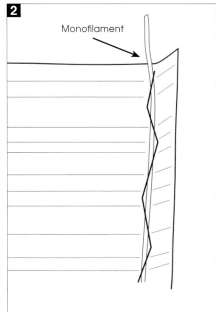

Monofilament

**Step 3** Trim the excess fabric close to the monofilament, taking care not to cut the stitches. The "bend" will now roll over the monofilament.

### SEWING MACHINE SETTINGS

**Stitch:** *Zigzag satin stitch*
**Stitch Width:** *0.6–0.8 mm*
**Stitch Length:** *0.5–1.0 mm*

**Step 4** Reset the machine for a satin stitch as indicated in the box at right. Sew over the monofilament and the edge; adjust the stitch width to cover the monofilament, if necessary. The needle should fall off the edge of the fabric on the right. The "bend" helps the satin stitch cover the "pokeys" (fabric threads that poke out of the satin stitching), because the cut edge rolls over the monofilament. If the monofilament isn't covered on the first pass, run the piece through the machine a second time.

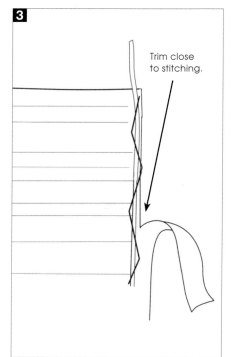

Trim close to stitching.

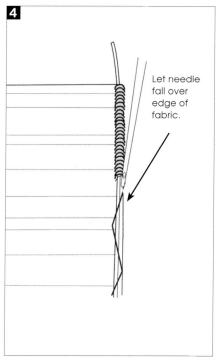

Let needle fall over edge of fabric.

➲ Imposing, but light as air, this ruffled "Chrysanthemum" evening cape is a stylish way to create drama without sacrificing warmth. The ruffles keep their edge with monofilament thread.

This gal is studying the gown to see if she's used the right amount of embellishment. The lavish use of decoration at the top is balanced by the long simple black column of skirt.

## Completing the ruffle

Once the prepleated or flat strip edge is finished and stiffened (using either the serger or the sewing machine method described previously), gather the opposite edge to make a ruffle of the required length. To do this, use either a ruffler attachment or your preferred machine-gathering method.

To attach the ruffle, follow steps 1 through 3 of "Knife-Pleated Edging" on page 135. What do you do with the ends of the monofilament? Because the ruffle has sweeps and curves, I bend the ends of the strip onto the seamline and stitch them, with the monofilament, into the seam when I sew on the ruffle; this works well aesthetically and saves aggravation. You can alternatively plan ahead and taper the end of the strip before gathering it.

⬆ The top of this ball gown is framed with a froth of mushroom-pleated ruffles, allowing the bodice to emerge as from a flower. To make mushroom pleats, you need to send the fabric to a commercial pleating house.

### POKEYS

*tip*

To conceal pokeys (the fabric threads that stick out of the satin stitching), use this trick from Sandra Betzina: Color the threads with permanent markers. Match the color of the marker to the thread used for the satin stitch.

# Knife-Pleated Edging

A narrow knife-pleated strip inserted into a seam gives a jaunty flourish to a garment or home accessory. You can insert a knife-pleated edging in an interior seam or at an edge, depending on the effect you're after. If you place it on an edge, you'll need a facing rather than a hem allowance. You can use ribbon or strips of fabric cut on the straight grain for a knife-pleated edging. The total strip length before pleating must be three times the length of the seam or edge you want to embellish, plus enough to finish the ends. If you're using fabric strips, you'll need seam allowances to sew them together before pleating.

The width of the strip depends on whether you choose to use ribbon or prefer to make the pleated edging out of fabric. Select a ribbon that is wide enough to extend from the seam with enough left over for a seam allowance so you can sew it on. To determine the width to cut fabric strips, first decide how far you want the pleated edging to extend from the seam, preferably $1/2$" to $5/8$" (1.3 to 1.5 cm). Then add a seam allowance and multiply by two. After the strips are cut and sewn together, press them in half lengthwise, right side out, before pleating.

To pleat the ribbon or the joined, pressed fabric strips, either use one of the pleating devices on the market (for small amounts, this is perfect) or send the material to a pleating house. If you send the material out, be sure to instruct the company not to cut it into sections but rather to pleat the ribbon or fabric in one continuous length. Joining individual sections together later is not fun, make no mistake about it!

⬆ Tiny knife-pleated edging creates a crisp accent, here decorated with beads.

Here's what you do to sew the pleated edging to your project. Before beginning, review positions 1 and 2 for the adjustable zipper foot on page 45. Construct your project to whatever stage makes sense for the way you plan to use the pleated edging. Add piping to the right side of the project, if you wish, for extra panache (see chapter 4).

### PARTS OF A PLEAT

**Leading edge:** The leading edge is the crease on the front side of the pleat. On the outer side is the pleat width, on the under side the pleat depth. The positions of the pleat width and depth are reversed on the back of the pleat.

**Pleat width:** The portion of the pleat that extends from the folded edge of the pleat to the fold of the next pleat.

**Depth:** The part of the pleat that is concealed when the pleat hangs correctly. The depth is two times the pleat return.

**Return:** The distance from the fold at the leading edge of the pleat to the back of pleat fold.

**Back of the Pleat:** The fold at the center of the pleat insertion, usually only visible on an accordion pleat.

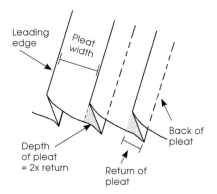

Leading edge

Pleat width

Depth of pleat = 2x return

Return of pleat

Back of pleat

**Step 1** Lay the project right side up. Lay the pleated edging right side down on top of it, with the seam allowances aligned and the finished edge of the pleated strip toward the interior of the project piece. Hand-baste the pleated edging to the project, sewing in the seam allowance.

**Step 2** Put the zipper foot to the right of the needle in position 1 (so the stitching is just to the right of the final seamline). With the project wrong side up (so the edging is against the feed dogs), sew the edging to the project with a long machine stitch.

**Step 3** To finish the seam, with right sides together and seamlines aligned, position the facing or adjacent piece under the edged piece. Pin. Then sew the seam with the zipper foot in position 2.

**Step 4** Now, if despite your best efforts, the edge of the pleating does not lie perfectly parallel to the seam (it happens!), don't despair. Don't rip out the seam either. Instead, after the piece is finished, tack down each corner with a bead as shown in the photo at right. The bead makes quite a nice edge and camouflages crooked work.

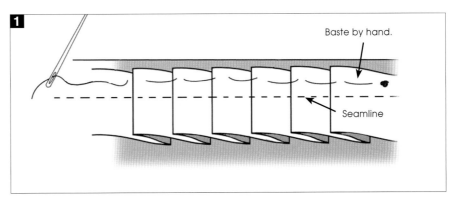

Baste by hand.

Seamline

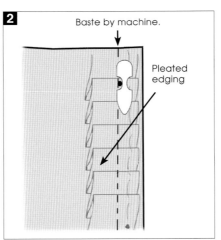

Baste by machine.

Pleated edging

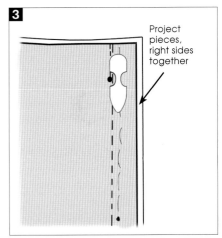

Project pieces, right sides together

**KEEP IT STRAIGHT!**
When hand-basting and machine-stitching, make sure the edge of the pleating is perfectly parallel to the seamline. If it's not, the end result will look very bad.

# Prairie Points

This technique is a quilting technique that I've adapted for clothing by reducing the scale of the prairie points and adding a flange. You can make this trim any size you like, so experiment to see how the technique works and then adjust the proportions to suit whatever you are making. If you work with striped fabric, the direction of the stripes will alternate, which is quite a cool effect. After you fold the prairie point strips, you sew them to a strip of bias fabric to create a flange so you can insert them into a seam, so be prepared with a long bias strip about 1" (2.5 cm) wide. The flange cleans up the edge of the prairie point strip and reduces the bulk going into a seam.

For best results, add prairie points to a piped seam. The piping will cover and neaten the overlapping edges of the points and the bias strip. Remember, the points will point away from the piping and lie on top of the adjacent piece when you are done, so if you are inserting this trim into an interior seam, think through which way you want them to point and sew the piping to the opposite section of the project. As a nifty touch on an interior seam, you can tack down some or all of the points with a bead to add more interest.

**Step 1** Cut strips for the prairie point trim as shown in the drawing, making them any width you desire and cutting on the lengthwise or crosswise straight grain. A good starting point is 3" to 4" (7 to 10 cm) wide. This width makes a petite prairie point, which works well on clothing (larger strips create quite a lovely effect for home furnishings). Whatever width you choose, make sure you can easily measure and divide it by 2 and by 4 so that you can mark a pattern of offset squares on it, as shown. The drawing shows how to set up a 4" (10 cm)-wide strip. Mark your strip on the wrong side of the fabric, cut the ends to be offset as shown, and cut the remaining horizontal lines to the center.

↻ Prairie points are a traditional quilting trim. When applied to the edges of evening fabrics, on a large scale, they appear exotic and chic. In this example, the vertical edge features the points as made. The diagonal edge shows the points opened and tacked to the side with beads.

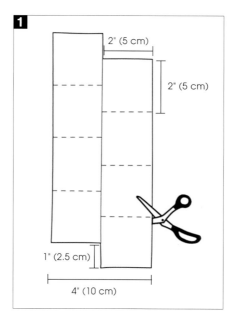

**1**

2" (5 cm)

2" (5 cm)

1" (2.5 cm)

4" (10 cm)

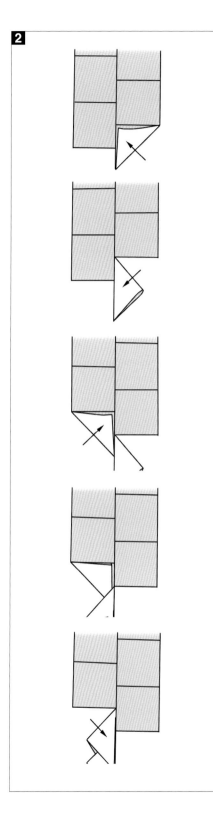

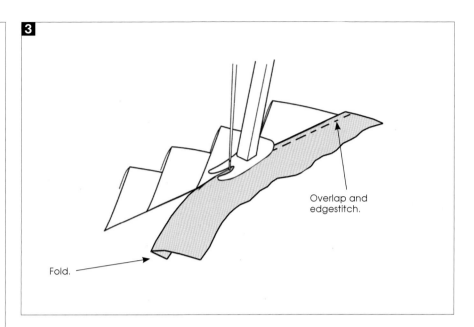

Overlap and edgestitch.

Fold.

**Step 2** Place the marked, cut strip wrong side up on your ironing board and fold it in the sequence shown in the drawings. Press as you fold. Repeat the sequence until the entire strip is folded. If you need more, make more; you can tuck the end of one strip into the beginning of the next when you sew them together in step 3.

**Step 3** Press under a narrow allowance on one edge of the bias strip. Lap the fold ever so slightly over the straight edge of the prairie point strip, as shown, and edgestitch them together.

**Step 4** Baste the strip to the project piece after you've sewn on the piping (but before you sew on the adjacent project piece). Be sure to orient the points toward the interior of the piece, placing the bias flange right side down over the seam allowance. Then stitch with the foot in position 1 (this is not a final seam). Construct the project seam as usual, trim, and press.

# Prairie Point Variations

Once you understand the basic process of making prairie points, you can make some cool variations: prairie point trim and prairie point piping. The base of the prairie point trim is bound with a bias strip so you can sew it to the face of a project. The base of the prairie point piping is enclosed between two bias strips so it is neat and clean and you can use it as an insertion without first sewing a separate piping to the seamline. You begin both the same way, which is just slightly different from the way the basic prairie points are folded.

⬆ In this detail shot of the slipcover, you can see the deep turquoise prairie points tacked down with beads.

In this example, I cut a 6" (15 cm)-wide strip, which, when pressed in half, is 3" (7.5 cm) wide. The individual prairie point units are 3" (7.5 cm) wide, too. If you'd like, you can play with these dimensions and make points that are larger or smaller. Cut the strip and mark the squares on it as shown in step 1 of "Prairie Points" on page 136.

↪ As you can see from this lavish slip-cover, embellishments are not for clothing alone. This chair features prairie points mixed with dazzling Swarovski crystals. The chair was commissioned and photographed by Swarovski.

**Step 1** The object of the game here is to make the points without creasing the second fold of each, so that they resemble soft petals. So, fold each square diagonally in half once and press, all the way up the strip, as shown.

**Step 2** Now, without pressing with an iron, fold each square in half diagonally again and rotate the alternate points into position, as shown, pinning them to each other to secure. (See step 2 of "Prairie Points" on page 137 for reference.)

**Step 3** Stitch the unit on the machine, ³/₈" (9 mm) away from the edge, as shown in the photo. Note the direction of the overlapping long ends of the points—it's easier to sew this unit if you're stitching off the points rather than onto them.

**Step 4** Now, cut 2" (5 cm)-wide bias strips for the next steps. For the prairie point trim, you need one strip per length of trim. For the prairie point piping, you need two strips per length of piping.

**Step 5** Lay a bias strip right side up. Place the prairie point unit right side down on it, aligning the cut edges. Sew together, following the previous line of stitching.

## Completing the prairie point trim

You'll use the bias strip attached in step 5 on the previous page to bind the edge of the prairie points. Once it's tidy, you can sew the trim wherever you like.

**Step 1** You want the prairie point unit to have a clean, even edge so the bias can wrap it smoothly. Working with a ruler and rotary cutter, trim the seam allowance to ¼" (6 mm) through all layers.

**Step 2** Press the bias strip away from the points, as shown; be careful not to crease the soft folds on the points.

**Step 3** Turn the unit over and fold the points up, wrapping the bias strip around the cut edge of the seam allowance. Press, again being sure not to crease the soft edge of the points.

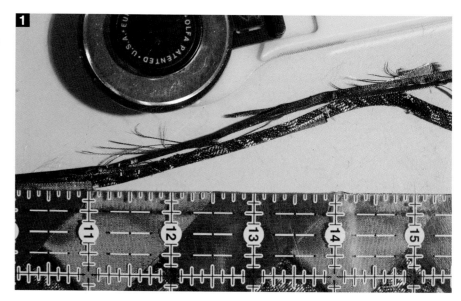

**Step 4** Put the adjustable zipper foot in position 2 and stitch in the ditch next to the bias through all layers, as shown in the photo.

**Step 5** Turn the trim over and cut away the excess bias strip, $1/8$" (3 mm) away from the machine stitching.

**Step 6** The finished trim will look as it does in the photo. Attach it to the surface of a garment or other project by hand with slipstitches or by machine, stitching in the ditch again.

**Step 7** To make a design variation, lay the trim right side up. Then open each point and tack its edge to the bias binding by hand.

## Completing the prairie point piping

You'll sandwich the raw edge of the prairie points between two bias strips to cover the seam allowance and create a flange. Then you can insert the points into a seam in the same way you would piping.

**Step 1** Complete steps 1 through 5 on page 139. Lay a second bias strip right side up. Place the prairie point unit point-side down on it, aligning the cut edges. Sew together, following the previous line of stitching.

**Step 2** Lift the top bias strip; you'll see that the points are sandwiched between the strips. Check that the overlapping point edges still lie smoothly. (If you see any little tucks, pick out the stitches, smooth the overlap, and resew.)

**Step 3** You want the prairie point unit to have a clean, even edge so that you'll be able to sew tightly against it to form a "piping" with the bias strips at the base of the points. Working with a ruler and rotary cutter, trim the seam allowance to ¼" (6 mm) through all layers.

**Step 4** Press one bias strip away from the points, as shown; be careful not to crease the soft folds on the points.

**Step 5** Turn the unit over and press the second bias strip away from the points and onto the first strip, as shown. Don't crease the soft folds on the points.

**Step 6** Put the zipper foot in Position 1. Sew the bias strips together, stitching right next to the enclosed seam allowance. It doesn't matter which bias strip is on top.

**Step 7** The finished piping looks the same on both sides. When you are ready to use it, insert it into a seam just as you would filled piping, positioning it so the enclosed edge of the prairie points will extend from the seam, as shown in the photo at far right, and sewing over the previous stitching on the bias flange (see "Basic Piped Seams," page 45).

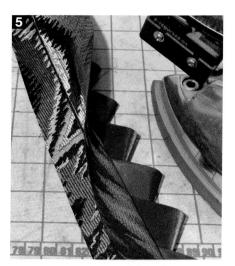

⬆ When the prairie point piping is inserted into a seam, the points make a dramatic edge, and the bias-covered base looks like narrow piping.

# Chinese Knots

Chinese knots are another embellishment that can be used for both apparel and home furnishings. They're classic choices for fastening that outré garment—the smoking jacket, a cool item for which smoking is not required! They're great on one-of-a-kind embellished jackets or vests, evening coats and wraps, or even casual vests or robes if you choose cord that has the right look for your fabric. In home furnishings, they are quite effective as tiebacks for draperies, as well as closures for slipcovers or pillow shams.

You can work with any type of cord or bias tubing for these knot closures. If you are working on a project where cost is an issue, buy less expensive fabric and put your money into the cord for the trimming—you'll elevate the look of the entire project. Make a sample before you purchase a lot of cord so you can make sure you have the right scale for wherever you're using the closure.

Tie a Chinese knot by following the sequence of steps shown in the drawings; work in the middle of a length of cord, leaving long tails to arrange decoratively on the surface of your project. After you have completed these steps, pull and massage the knot to form a round shape.

Arrange the tails however you wish on your project and sew them on by hand. Be sure to plan a way to conceal the cut ends under the curlicues of your design, thread them to the back of the work in a place where they won't be obvious (see "Finishing the Trim Ends" on page 166), or finish them by tying in small knots so that they become part of the effect. Use a second length of cord to create a decorative loop on the opposite side of your garment (or whatever you're making) for fastening the knot.

You'll find other inspirational ideas for making decorative frogs and knots in the terrific book, *Ashley's Book of Knots* by Clifford W. Ashley. This book is the Sears catalog of knots, with more than 7,000 drawings of more than 3,900 knots. If you were deserted on an island, this book and a heap of twine is what you would wish for.

↻ Chinese knots, also referred to as "monkey fist" knots, provide a beautiful way to make buttons that match a project. They also are a lovely embellishment when combined with beads or passementerie (see page 160).

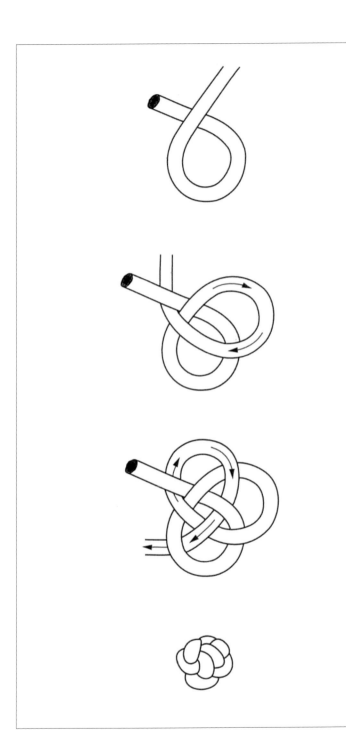

**FROG MEDALLIONS**

If you pull the Chinese knot flat instead of massaging it into a ball, it can be the medallion part of a frog closure. Then tie a round knot or make a fastening loop in one of the tails.

⬆ You can create a lavish surface treatment like this only after the welt pocket has been set in and the lapel is finished. Then is the time to add decorative knots and passementerie.

# Tassels

Tassels provide movement and weight to eveningwear and daywear alike.
In the middle ages, it was believed that tassels scared away evil spirits and, if worn, kept them off the wearer. (Apparently, evil spirits couldn't climb through tassels.) In modern times, tassels are used to decorate, weight, and add movement to whatever they adorn. When planning how to use tassels, I generally decide to integrate the cord on which they hang into the design of the overall embellishment, and once that embellishment is done, I construct the tassel directly onto the piece. The classic tassel is the single layer tassel, but you can create more interest by making a multi-layered tassel. By making your own tassels, you can save money and have exactly the tassel you need to match the rest of the piece.

## Single-layer tassel

There are four parts to a tassel: the cord, the knob, the waist, and the skirt. The easiest way to make a tassel is to begin with a length of cord and a quantity of chainette fringe. Tie a knot in the cord, sew the band along the top of the fringe to the cord below the knot, wrapping it around as much as you like, then invert it over the knot you tied and bind it below the knot. Voilà, the knot becomes the tassel knob, the dangling fringe the skirt. Once the tassel is finished, you can embellish its waist with a string of seed beads if you wish.

The thickness of the tassel depends on how much fringe is wrapped around the cord. For our purposes, we will discuss tassels made from a 16" (40.5 cm) piece of chainette fringe (measured along the top edge), which makes a tassel with a knob approximately 1¼" (3 cm) thick. The fringe can be any length you like from top to bottom. It should be about twice the knob height plus whatever skirt length you want; you can cut off any excess length at the bottom of the skirt when you're finished. This is all hard to visualize from words, so look through the drawings to see how it works. The drawings at right show the parts of a tassel and the parts of the fringe—familiarize yourself with these because they are referred to throughout the tassel-making directions.

**Step 1** First make a knot in the end of a piece of cord. The knot will become the inside of the knob and keep the tassel from pulling loose. You'll wrap the fringe onto the cord with this knot pointing up and the fringe strands pointing down. Position the knotted cord and fringe as shown in the drawing, with the top edge of the fringe foundation snug against the knot, and whipstitch one end of the foundation band at the top of the fringe to the cord.

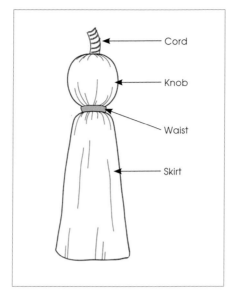

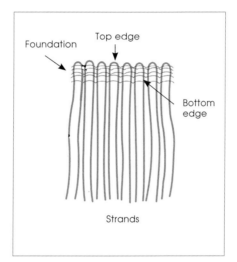

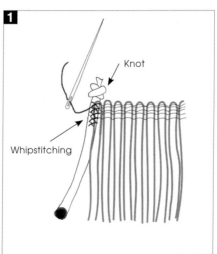

⬆ The center tassel has a mold, which shapes the knob and gives this tassel a different appearance than the other two (see page 158). The knob on the right-hand tassel has a beaded cage (see page 155).

## ABOUT FRINGE

You'll find rayon chainette fringe in most fabric and trim shops. Making tassels from fringe saves you the trouble of wrapping fine cord or yarn around a card and then tying one end and cutting the other. The fringe is already secured at one edge with a "foundation" of stitches, and the individual strands will not shed over time. Fringe is also easy to control while you're constructing the tassel.

Fringe comes in lengths from 2" (5 cm) to about 30" (76 cm), so you can make any length of tassel you desire. The foundation of the fringe is formed with either three or five rows of stitching that hold the strands together. The three-row foundation will make a rounder knob, and the five-row foundation will produce a more oblong knob, but the method of construction is the same. The strands may be secured with rows of temporary chain stitches at intervals below the foundation; leave these in place until you're ready to begin attaching the fringe to the tassel cord, because they keep the strands from tangling.

With this fringe method of tassel construction, you can easily add a tassel to finish a tie or cord on a project. Think how nice these tassels would look as finishes on some of those piping techniques you learned in chapter 4.

**Step 2** Wrap the fringe foundation snugly around the cord, making sure the top edge remains even and is resting against the bottom of the knot. After you have wrapped all the fringe around the cord, whipstitch the loose end of the foundation to the wrapped section.

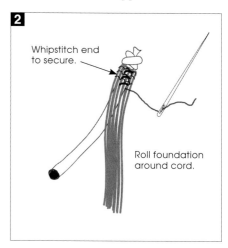

Whipstitch end to secure.

Roll foundation around cord.

### ROLL TO WRAP

The easiest way to wrap the fringe is to lay it flat and roll up the cord into it.

**Step 3** Take several stab stitches through the roll of foundation, making sure the needle also passes through the cord. These stitches will secure the fringe so it doesn't pull away later.

**Step 4** Rethread the needle, attaching it to the bottom edge of the rolled foundation. Tightly wrap the thread many times around the strands of the fringe, just below the bottom edge of the foundation, to pull the strands tightly against the cord. The thread will "fall off" the roll of foundation, just as it should. Take a few stitches to secure; knot the thread and cut off the excess.

**Step 5** If the cord extends beyond the exposed knot more than a little bit, cut it off. Rethread the needle and take a couple of stitches through the knot. These stitches will keep the knot secure over time. Keep the threaded needle attached to the tassel while you do the next step.

**Step 6** Grasp the unknotted end of the cord and invert the tassel. It's now right side up, with the fringe strands hanging down over the wrapped foundation and the knot. Evenly distribute the strands around the tassel with a blunt needle or one of those plastic hair-lift combs to conceal the wrapped foundation and knot. Pull firmly down on the strands to set them. The needle and thread are still attached to the knot and will be hanging down among all these strands.

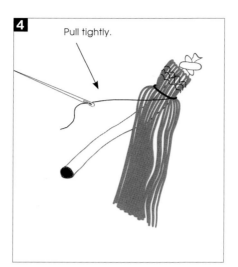

4 — Pull tightly.

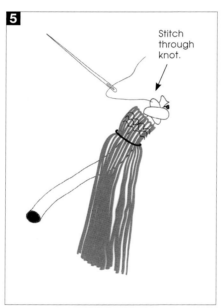

5 — Stitch through knot.

6 — Thread in needle

**Step 7** You may wish to attach the loose end of the cord to a "third hand" or have someone hold the cord for you while you form the waist of the tassel. Bring the needle to the outside of the fringe below the knot and grasp the strands below the knot in one hand. Wrap the thread around the strands once to define the knob and waist. Pass the needle under the beginning of the thread, pull the needle down, and then wrap several times in the opposite direction. The change in direction when wrapping prevents a dent in the waist where the thread exits the strands. Stitch and knot to secure; insert the needle through the skirt and cut off the excess thread.

Wrap strands once; change direction and wrap several times more.

**THREE HANDS ARE BETTER** *tip*

A third hand is anything you can firmly attach the cord to so you can put some tension on it—a new or antique sewing bird that can grasp the cord in its beak, or a pincushion on a clamp affixed to your table are the usual forms. If the cord is long enough, tie it to a doorknob or the back of a chair.

**Step 8** Conceal the thread at the waist by covering it with seed beads. Rethread the needle (or a beading needle, depending on the size of the beads). Pull the needle and thread up in the center of the skirt (A), exiting on the waist (B). The knot will be concealed in the skirt.

**Step 9** String onto the needle and thread as many beads as necessary to go around the waist of the tassel. Pull the beads around the waist and then pass the needle again through the first bead on the strand (A). Pass the needle through the tassel at the waist, coming out on the opposite side of the waist. Pull the thread snug but not too tight, otherwise a dip will form in the waist.

**Step 10** Whipstitch over the strand of beads to keep it from falling off the waist, making sure the stitches fall between the beads. To finish, knot the thread and cut off the excess.

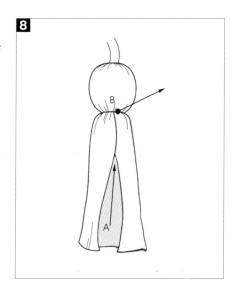

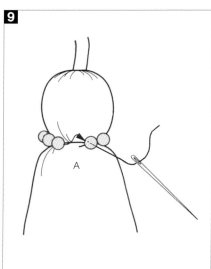

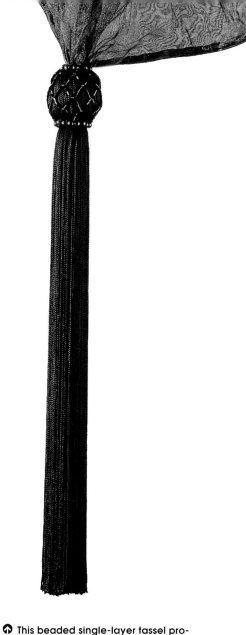

**SEED BEADS**

When putting beads around the waist of the tassel, use a size 5° seed bead. This bead is about ¹/₈" (3 mm) in diameter. For this size tassel, you will need 20 to 22 seed beads.

↥ This beaded single-layer tassel provides weight to the end of an organza shawl, helping to control the way the shawl hangs when worn. It adds movement and a little sparkle as well.

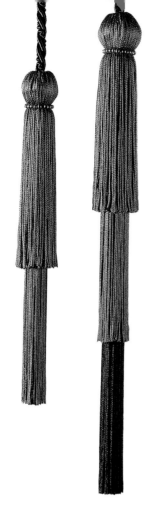

## Double- and triple-layer tassels

These variations on the single-layer tassel are made with multiple layers of different lengths of fringe, which create an attractive effect, especially if you choose different colors. In the directions for making these, I refer to the bottom layer as layer 1, the middle layer as layer 2 (for the triple-layer tassel), and the top layer as the top; you can see these in the drawing at right.

Layer 1 is wrapped on first, with succeeding layers wrapped on top of it. For the single-layer tassel (see page 146), you use a 16" (40.5 cm) piece of fringe (measured along the foundation) to create a 1¹/₄" (3 cm)-thick knob. For these variations, you also use a total of 16" (40.5 cm) of fringe, but it will be divided among the layers. The fringe strands can be any length you like. Only the top layer is inverted for these; look through the directions to see how the fringe is applied so you can judge the length to work with for each layer.

For a double-layer tassel, use 7" (18 cm) of fringe for layer 1, and 9" (23 cm) for the top layer. For a triple-layer tassel, use 3" (7.5 cm) of fringe for layer 1, 5" (12.5 cm) for layer 2, and 8" (20 cm) for the top layer. Notice that the underlayers have less fringe and the succeeding upper layers have more; it takes more fringe to cover the circumference as the tassel gets thicker. More fringe around the upper layers guarantees coverage and balance.

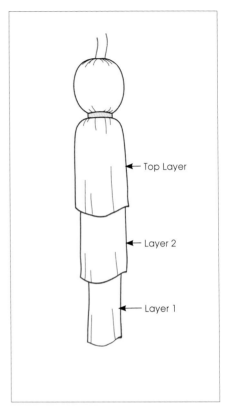

Top Layer

Layer 2

Layer 1

⬑ Double- and triple-layer tassels add complexity to your designs. You can introduce different colors from the garment or accessory into the tassel, to tie the whole piece together.

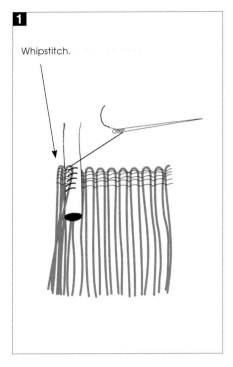

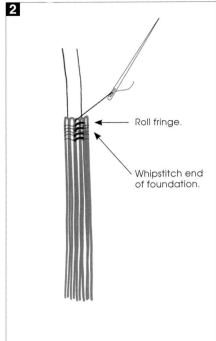

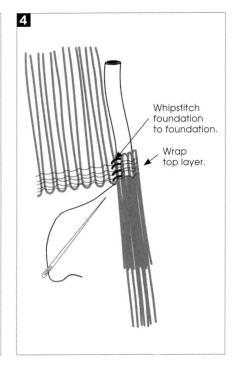

**Step 1** For this style of tassel, you don't knot the cord. Position the cord and fringe layer 1 as shown. Whipstitch the end of the fringe foundation to the cord.

**Step 2** Wrap layer 1 around the cord, and then whipstitch the loose end of the foundation to the wrapped section. Pass the needle and thread back and forth through the wrapped foundation and cord several times.

**Step 3** If you are making a triple-layer tassel, repeat steps 1 and 2 to add layer 2 on top of layer 1.

**Step 4** Position the top layer next to the wrapped tassel, as shown, with the strands pointing away from the other layer(s) and the foundations overlapping. Whipstitch the end of the top layer foundation in place; then wrap the top layer around the tassel.

**SPECIAL EFFECTS**
You can tie the upper layers of multiple-layer tassels to create a series of knobs that looks nice against the contrasting color of the lower layers. Braiding on the upper layers of a tassel, or making braids on the single-layer tassel, is also cool.

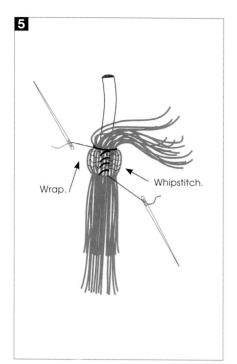

**5**

Wrap.

Whipstitch.

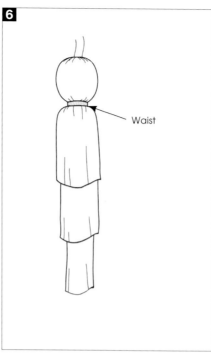

**6**

Waist

**Step 5** Whipstitch the loose end of the top foundation to the wrapped area to secure; knot the thread and cut off the excess. Rethread the needle and attach it to the top layer foundation right next to the strands. Tightly wrap the thread many times around the strands to pull them snug against the cord, as shown in the drawing. The thread will "fall off" the roll of foundation, just as it should. Take a few stitches to secure; knot the thread and cut off the excess.

**Step 6** Fold the top layer fringe down and comb the strands into place, evenly distributing them around the circumference of the tassel. Rethread the needle and follow step 7 of "Single-layer tassel" on page 150 to form the waist.

**TRIMMING THE TASSEL SKIRTS**
Rayon chainette steams out really well. After you've completed a tassel, steam it with your iron. Then shake it to let the strands hang. Even up the ends simply by cutting them straight across with scissors. For multiple-layer tassels, trim the top layer and work down, pulling the other layers aside while letting the layer to be trimmed hang alone.

Trim layer 1 (the bottom layer) so that the visible part is $1/4$" to $3/8$" (6 mm to 1 cm) longer than the visible portion of the other layers. This will make the visible portion the layers each appear to be the same length. If the visible portions were all the same, layer 1 would look shorter than the upper layers. When you make a tiered skirt, for example, you make the exposed portion of the bottom tier $1/2$" (1.3 cm) longer than the upper tiers for the same reason. In the picture-framing trade, this is called "weighting" the bottom portion of a mat.

## Bead mesh cages for knobs

Bead mesh "cages" are nifty for covering the knob of a tassel. It's smart to consider your first one a sample. You have to make it over a tassel knob, but you may decide the bead size isn't right or your first attempt may not be as neat as you wish. There is some stress on the thread, so use Nymo or silamide, which has the right strength. If you use Nymo, press each length to keep it from kinking.

**Step 1** Attach a row of beads around the tassel waist following steps 8 and 9 for "Single-layer tassel" on page 151. This is the home row, and it must have an even number of beads. Rethread your needle with a 72" (1.8 m) strand of thread; double it and knot the ends together. (Bead mesh eats up thread, so give yourself lots of extra.) Pull the needle up through the skirt of the tassel and exit at the waist, as you did when applying the home row, but come out between two of the beads (A).

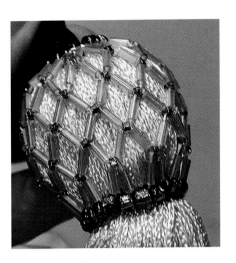

A bead mesh cage gives the knob of the tassel definition and enables you to incorporate beads into the tassel. You can make the cage from seed and bugle beads or entirely from seed beads. The method of working is the same for both.

**1**

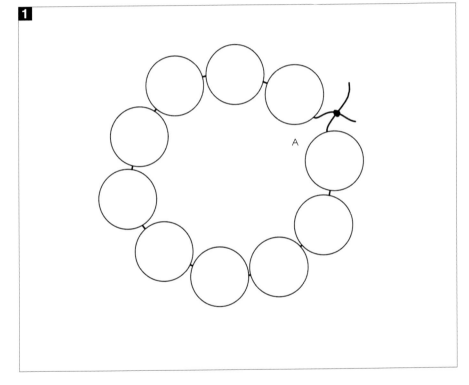

A

*tip* **THREADING BEADS**
There will be quite a bit of thread passing through the holes of the beads, so whenever possible, work with beads that have slightly larger holes. You can visually compare the beads or ask the person at the bead store for a recommendation. Also, a small needle (size 12 or 13) is useful, but threading small needles can be a pain. Most people are comfortable with a size 10 needle.

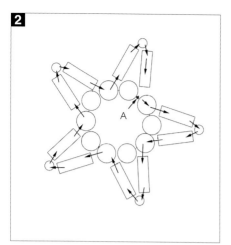

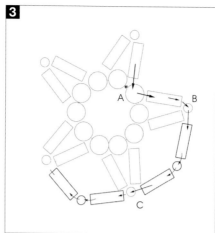

⬆ Pin each bugle-seed-bugle bead unit into the tassel knob to help you create the mesh shape.

**Step 2** Pass the needle through one bead in the home row. To create the first row of the mesh, pass the needle through one bugle bead, one seed bead (of any size, but the teeny ones work well for bead mesh—experiment!), and another bugle bead and push them onto the thread to create a "unit." Skip one bead on the home row, pass the needle through the next bead, and then through another bugle, seed, and bugle bead to create another unit. Repeat this threading pattern all around, as shown, bringing the needle out through the last bugle bead above the starting point (A).

As you work, you can pin these units onto the knob with straight pins, as shown in the photo at above. This will help you shape the mesh with the correct thread tension, which should be somewhat loose. Tight tension will cause the mesh to wear prematurely and makes the knob "crunchy" (for lack of a better word). As always, practice will tell you how to regulate the tension!

**Step 3** Pass the needle through the first bead in the home row again (next to A), then pass it up through the first bugle bead and the seed bead in the first unit (B). To create the next mesh row, add a bugle bead, seed bead, and bugle bead to the thread and pass the needle through the seed bead of the next unit in the first row, as shown (C). Continue in this manner to add a bugle bead, seed bead, and bugle bead between each of the units of the first row. You'll end ready to join a bugle-seed-bugle unit to seed bead B.

As you work around the tassel, move the pins from the first mesh row to pin up the seed beads of the second row, as shown in the photo above.

 **KEEPING TRACK**

Here's a tip for avoiding confusion as you pass the needle through the seed beads. Each seed bead on the uppermost row forms the tip of an upside-down bugle-bead V, which to you should mean "Very good, you may continue." The seed beads you should not use are in the middle of a bugle-bead X, meaning "No! Don't use this one." This trick may be hokey, but it works.

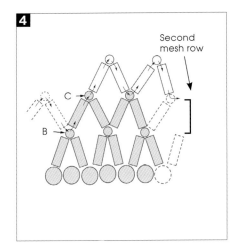

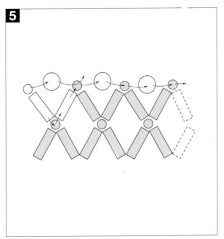

**Step 4** Referring to the drawing above, pass the needle through seed bead B, then pass it up through the first bugle bead and the seed bead in the first unit of the second mesh row (C). Then create the third mesh row in the same way you created the second one. Be sure to keep moving the pins up as work progresses to avoid confusion as to which seed bead to pass the needle through. Repeat this step as needed until the pointed units extend to the top of the knob.

**Step 5** When the mesh is tall enough, go around one more time, adding a single bead between each point of the previous row. This bead can be similar to one of the beads in the home row or another seed bead.

**Step 6** Then, to close the "cage," pull the thread taut through the last row, drawing the beads close to the tassel cord, as shown in the photo. Pass the needle through the first bead in this row two or three times, then knot the thread, slide the needle through the knob, and cut off the excess thread.

⊙ Use pins to hold the second mesh row in place on the tassel knob.

⊙ Larger, contrast beads in the top row add a flourish to the beaded mesh cage.

## Tassel molds

A tassel mold is a piece of wood or other material that gives shape to the knob of the tassel. The tassel fringe hangs from the mold, which can either be covered by the fringe or by other materials. Molds can be part of the tassel itself or slipped onto the cord of the finished tassel.

You can use many things as tassel molds—thread spools, macramé beads, baby's teething beads, even actual tassel molds themselves (when you can find them, and then if you can afford them). If you choose macramé beads or other wooden shapes, look for large holes. You can also cover molds, using two techniques: wrapping and upholstering.

### Wrapping a mold

You can achieve interesting effects by wrapping a tassel mold with ribbons, cords, or even beads strung on thread. Once the mold is wrapped, simply slide it onto the tassel cord; affix with a little glue, if you wish.

To wrap with ribbons or cords, just keep passing the material through the hole, either overlapping or abutting the strands to cover the mold. Make a few stitches to tack the ends (or put some glue inside the hole), and you're finished.

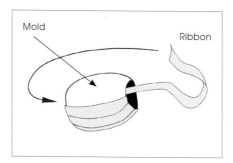

To wrap with beads, just pass the beading thread through the hole and string beads onto the thread to cover the outside of the mold. If you string one fewer bead on every other wrap, it helps to distribute the beaded thread evenly around the mold. You can even make bead mesh cages around molds for a cool effect.

### Upholstering a mold

Not much fabric is required to cover a tassel mold, so this technique provides a good way to use the scraps of that expensive fabric you have been saving.

**Step 1** Measure the circumference of the tassel mold and the length of the mold to figure out how wide and long to make the upholstery casing. Add a little extra for seam allowances—$1/2$" (1.3 cm) to each dimension is plenty.

**Step 2** Cut this piece out of the fabric, on the bias (unless you have a stripe that you want to have travel around the piece). Bias fabric will finish better around the contours of the mold.

**Step 3** Fold the piece lengthwise in half, wrong side out. Sew the lengthwise seam. Slip the tassel cord through the mold and then the casing, and secure to the mold with a dot of glue.

**Step 4** By hand, sew a running stitch around the end of the casing closest to the mold.

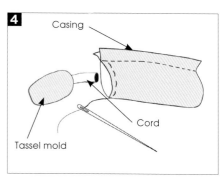

**Step 5** Pull up the running stitch to fit the casing tightly around the cord. Stitch the casing to the cord to secure.

**Step 6** With your fingers, turn the casing right side out and ease it down over the mold. By hand, sew a running stitch along the open end of the casing, and then pull it snug against the mold, poking the seam allowance into the hole of the mold with the needle.

➲ The oversized tassel at one end of this evening wrap adds drama, and its weight balances the cuff at the other end.

# *P*assementerie

Passementerie, from the French word for ornamental braid, is the art of making elaborate decorative trims and edgings from thin cord. Passementerie is beautiful and sophisticated, but it's a pain to plan and mark an intricate arrangement on your fabric. If you want a design that repeats or mirror-images on a garment or accessory, you need some sort of guide to follow. Once you know the cool trick I used to make the velvet cape shown at right, you can do similar work yourself without ever picking up chalk or a tracing wheel.

When I first began my designing career, I was making evening vests and needed to find a way to make passementerie mirror images match (I'm somewhat dyslexic). I hit upon the idea of using yardage trim (called braid in the "trade") as a base for additional cord and bead embellishment. This trim is structured with a small pattern "unit" that repeats regularly. When you apply the trim to a fabric surface, the repeating unit provides a consistent measuring device that you can use to guide all the rest of the ornamentation you add. If you're just

↥ Using the repeating pattern units in the base trim as a placement guide, I was able to create this complex mirrored design without first marking anything on the fabric.

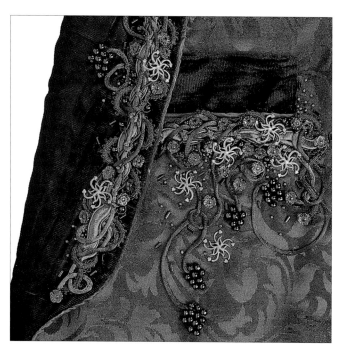

↥ The passemeterie on the lapels establishes the theme of this composition, and the chest pocket passementerie provides the variation.

↥ A touch of passementerie on the cuff of this smoking jacket carries the theme of embellishment of lapel and pocket to complete the look.

creating a single, free-form medallion
or band, the trim is a handy base, but if
you want to duplicate your arrangement
of cord and beads—say, as a border—or
reverse it on opposite sides of center
front, you can work out the first area and
then easily recreate it by using the same
number of "units" for each correspond-
ing detail.

I had to answer two questions to make
this technique viable: What do I do with
the ends of the trim, and how do I make
it not look like I just sewed down some
purchased trim? Answering these questions resulted in the particular style that
I became known for as my career and
reputation grew. For the first, I figured
out how to separate the cords that form
the trim and pull them individually
to the wrong side of the work. For the
second, I went for the "more is more"
effect, and embellished the trim with
additional cords and beads, practically
burying the original trim and creating
an elaborate pattern at the same time.

➲ On this evening cape, the sweep of
midnight blue iridescent velvet is set
off by lavish black passementerie.

## Fabrics and materials

This embellishment technique works on all types of fabrics (although I haven't tried it on leather), so fabric choice is a matter of personal taste.

I like to interline with felt. Wool is best, but it can be difficult to find, so you can substitute acrylic if necessary. The felt lies underneath the embellishment, creating a richer texture. The felt also provides a base onto which to stitch the ends of the cords and a base to knot off threads and such. It also supports the weight of the embellishment on the fashion fabric.

Any thread will do, but I prefer a cotton-wrapped polyester or 100 percent polyester thread. When threading the needle, double your thread for strength. Nymo thread is good when you're making a garment that needs to withstand heavy use—such as skating costumes or stage clothing. I also use it when I make bead dangles or fringe. All the stitching in the photos is done with a heavy contrasting thread so that you can see it, but you don't want to see it in real life, so use matching thread.

You'll also need a packing/sacking needle like the one shown here, which you can find in the repair packs of needles found in the notions section of every sewing store and even in many general merchandise stores. This needle has a large eye and a wide, curved point. The large eye accepts the cords of the trim base and also the rattail, and when the curved point is inserted through the fabric you're embellishing, it separates the woven or knit threads instead of piercing them and so allows the cords to pass through without marring the fabric. This needle allows you to pull cords to the back of the trim and interweave the rattail into the cord later.

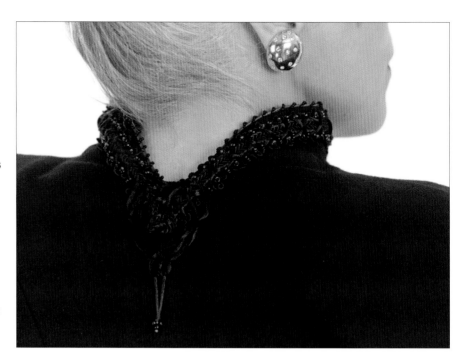

⬆ Passementerie can embellish an "architectural" detail of a garment, like the V on the back of this wool jacket.

The most important material for this technique is the trim that forms the base of the embellishment. I call this material "trim" for a reason. It's made of decorative cords that are arranged in patterns—those repeating units I mentioned earlier—and chain-stitched into place (you can see both sides in the photo at top left on the facing page). On the right side of the trim, the stitches look like regular machine straight stitches. On the wrong side, they're interlocking loops. If you release the chain stitch, the cords are easy to untwine and separate, which you need to do in order to pull them to the back of the fabric you're embellishing.

There are many, many trims with this type of structure, and they come in a variety of widths and patterns. To demonstrate this technique, I use white trims, but you can find a wide range of colors. Because they are made of cotton and rayon, you can dye them, too. The number of rows of chain stitching varies with the trim, from two rows down the center on a narrow trim up to as many as six or seven rows on a wide one.

⬆ With a little practice, you'll be able to pull heavy thread or decorative cords through satin with a packing/sacking needle without snagging the satin.

⬆ The top row shows the front (right side) of the trim; the bottom row shows the back (wrong side). You can see the rows of chain stitching best on the back. This particular trim is held together by three rows of chain stitching.

When you are choosing a trim for your base, consider the scale of the repeating unit to make sure it suits the type of embellishment you want to add (you'll understand this better after you read through this demonstration), and make sure it is held together with chain stitches. On the material I call braid, the cords are intertwined or woven; there are no chain stitches, and you can't easily separate the cords, so it doesn't work for this technique.

Traditional passementerie is made with fine cords such as soutache and gimp. Soutache is the flat, skinny, thread-wrapped cord often seen on military uniforms. Gimp is the thin, round cord from which many upholstery trims are fashioned, including the ones I use as a base for this technique. You can use both for my technique, but I usually add rattail because it gives a lot of impact (see photo, page 17). It is a satin-finished cord readily available in notions and trims shops. It comes in two thicknesses: one is 1/8" (3 mm), and the thinner one (called mouse tail) is 1/16" (2 mm). It comes in lots of colors. Both sizes of rattail are good to swirl and twine into embellishments to supplement the trim that forms the base

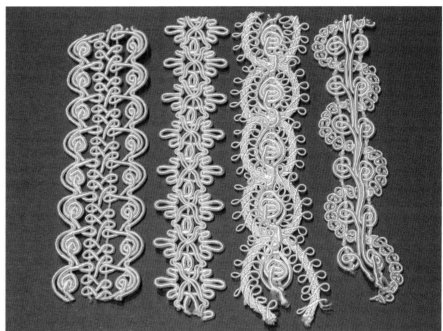

⬆ These are just a few of the trim patterns you can use for passementerie embellishment. Three of these are arranged symmetrically on both edges; the one on the right has an offset pattern. Each type offers different embellishment possibilities.

of my passementerie technique.

Any kind of beads or other ornaments are fair game for passementerie embellishment. I've integrated watch parts, nuts and bolts, and feathers—your choices are a matter of personal taste.

## Choosing landmarks

You must be thoughtful about where on the trim you place the hand-stitches when you sew it to your fabric. You can't simply affix it with a running stitch or slipstitch, because doing so would close up space you'll want for weaving in the rattail or adding other embellishments. And because you rely on the repeating pattern unit to guide the embellishment, you need to position your hand-stitches in consistent positions and then remember where you place them so that later you'll know where they are. I call these stitch locations "landmarks."

On the trim shown below, I have decided to use the circular portions of the design as the landmarks. These are on the rows of chain stitching and are spaced at regular intervals. Your trim will likely be different, so use your discretion as to which parts to use as landmarks, but make sure they are on the rows of chain stitching.

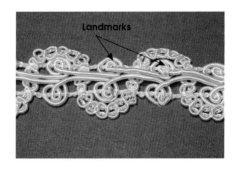

Landmarks

⬆ The circular elements paired along this trim are regularly spaced and easy to remember as landmarks.

## Sewing on the trim

**Step 1** First determine how much trim you'll need. Measure the length of the space you plan to embellish and add 2" to 3" (5 to 7.5 cm) at each end for finishing. Cut your trim to this total length. If you are embellishing two identical areas, cut the trim the same for each. If the design will mirror-image, make sure a nonsymmetrical trim like the one shown is cut correctly for that to happen.

**Step 2** Pin the trim into position on your piece, leaving an excess amount at each end loose so you can finish it later. The pins in the fabric show the ends of the embellishment area.

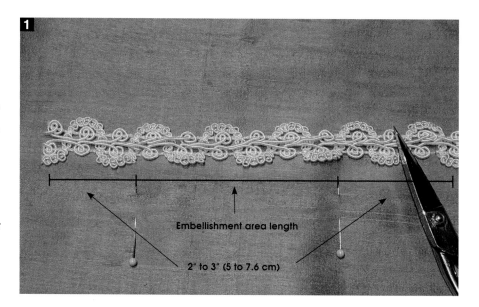

Embellishment area length

2" to 3" (5 to 7.6 cm)

**CHECK THE LANDMARKS** *tip*
Make sure your chosen landmarks are at the beginning and end of the measured "embellishment" section of the trim when you cut.

*tip* **LOCKING THE CHAIN**
If there isn't a landmark on some of the chain stitching at the end of your embellishment area, lock the next nearest landmark with four backstitches. Make sure you're working inside the embellishment area.

**Step 3** To begin attaching the trim, you need to secure the landmarks at one end of the embellishment area with a few backstitches. I call this a "locking stitch" because it secures the cords of the trim to the chain stitches so the trim doesn't unravel as you embellish it or when you secure the loose ends to the fabric. Follow the sequence of photos at right, making each stitch over one of the cords in the landmark and stitching right over the chain stitches.

First bring the needle and thread up between the cords on the chain stitch (photo 3a). Insert the needle in front of that cord (photo 3b). Pull the thread taut over the cord to close the stitch, and bring the needle up again on the far side of the next cord (photo 3c). Insert the needle again in front of the second cord and pull the thread taut (photo 3d). Repeat this process two more times, to make a total of four locking stitches. Then repeat the whole process for the other landmark (or landmarks) at this end of the embellishment area. Be sure to lock every row of chain stitching (photo 3e). Don't knot or cut the thread.

**Step 4** Now you're ready to tack down the rest of the trim. Make one backstitch in the middle of the next landmark.

**Step 5** Continue, making just one backstitch on each remaining landmark and working in a zigzag pattern all along the trim to the other end of the embellishment area. "Tack down" means just that—you don't have to make this stitching withstand gale-force winds.

**Step 6** At the opposite end of the embellishment area, make another set of four locking stitches for each row of chain stitching. End with the needle on the wrong side of the fabric, knot the thread, and cut off the excess. (The excess can be used to attach the cord ends later.)

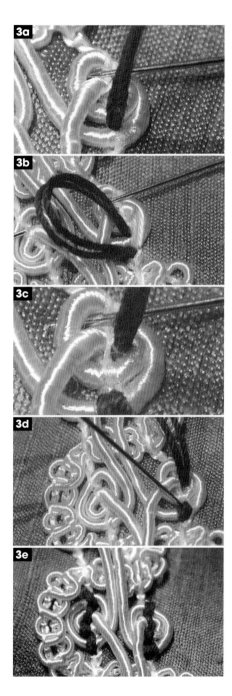

Stitch in a zigzag sequence

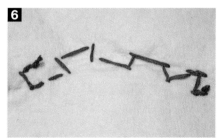

### UNRAVELING CHAIN STITCH

Chain stitch is made with one continuous thread, and there is a definite way to unravel it. As you can see in the photo below, each loop of the chain feeds out of the previous one. The loops are shaped like teardrops. The chain will unravel from the loop end toward the pointed end of the teardrops.

To unravel the chain stitch, simply pull the "tail" away from the end loop, which will slide out from the next loop. Keep pulling, and you'll see a chain reaction.

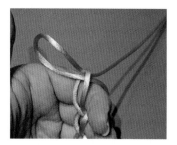

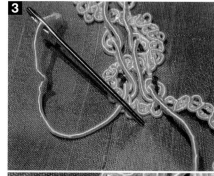

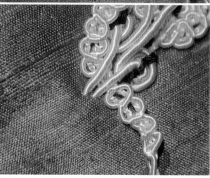

## Finishing the trim ends

**Step 1** On the trim, at both ends of the embellishment area, cut each row of chain stitching next to the locking stitches; be sure to cut outside the embellishment area.

**Step 2** Next, unravel the chain stitching at the loose ends of the trim so you can separate the cord ends and pull them to the wrong side of the fabric (see the sidebar at right). If your trim has smaller multicord elements like the one in the photo, you don't need to unravel them unless they won't fit in the eye of the packing needle. When you have the cords separated, you're ready to begin the embellishment—that's where the creativity comes in.

**Step 3** To begin the embellishment, I usually thread the cord ends one at a time onto the packing/sacking needle and pull each through to the back of the work. My feeling is that these cords don't provide much bang for the buck, but you can use them as part of the embellishment, if you wish. Insert the needle close to the trim as shown in the first photo above, unless you want a bridge of cord as part of your design. You can see in the second photo above how neat it looks once the cord ends are no longer visible on the right side of the fabric.

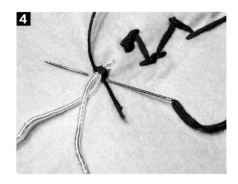

**Step 4** After pulling the cord to the back, stitch it to the felt backing. Use the same thread used for sewing on the trim and just whipstitch over the cord a few times to keep it from pulling back to the front. Then cut the excess about $^1/_4$" (6 mm) from the stitches. You can secure a couple of cords at once, as shown.

**Step 5** If your separated trim ends include a multicord piece like the one in the photos, arrange the end of this piece on the right side of your work in whatever design you'd like, and pin it in place. Thread the end through the packing/sacking needle and pull it to the back of the work wherever is appropriate for your design. Leave the portion on the right side of the work pinned in place and stitch the end to the felt on the wrong side.

## Adding the embellishments

**Step 1** Now you're ready to incorporate the rattail. To get the required length of rattail for the job, measure between the ends of the trim and multiply the measurement by four. Cut a piece of rattail cord that length.

**Step 2** You'll work with the packing/sacking needle to weave the rattail into the trim, but before you thread the needle, you need to thin the end of the cord. Follow the sequence of photos at right to cut the core out of the rattail, and then thread the needle.

To begin, look at the cut end of the rattail and find the core (photo 2a). Grab the core with your thumbnail and index finger and pull out about 1" (2.5 cm) (photo 2b). Trim off the pulled-out core (photo 2c). Compress the cover fibers at the end of the rattail between your thumb and index finger. Then set the eye of the needle down over the fibers, forcing them into the eye (photo 2d). Pull about $^3/_8$" (1 cm) of rattail—no more than that—through the needle eye (photo 2e).

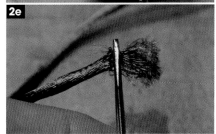

## SEWING DOWN THE CORD

Here's an easy stitch with which to invisibly secure the rattail cord to the fabric. To begin, thread your regular hand-sewing needle with thread to match the cord and insert it from the wrong side of the work right next to the cord, on the outside of the curve.

Pull up the thread. Now put the needle back into the fabric, just catching the side of the cord.

Pull the stitch closed. Continue in this way, making stitches about ¹/₄" to ³/₈" (6 mm to 1 cm) apart.

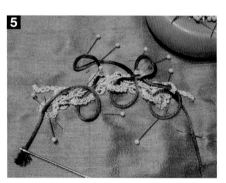

**Step 3** To begin, pin the unthinned end of the rattail onto the fabric, close to one end of the trim.

**Step 4** Leading with the eye of the needle, weave the rattail under one part of the trim near the end.

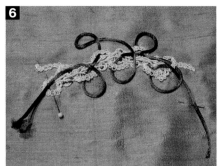

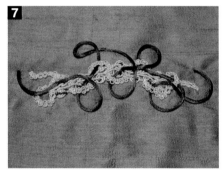

**Step 5** Continue, weaving the rattail back and forth under the loose parts of the trim, between your landmarks. Pin as you go, adjusting the cord arrangement until it satisfies you.

**Step 6** After you've woven the length of rattail cord through the trim, sew down the cord, following the instructions in the sidebar at left. When you are finished, the cord will appear to float on the right side of the work.

**Step 7** On the right side of your embellishment, decide where you want the ends of the rattail to disappear. Thread each end through the packing/sacking needle and pull it to the wrong side.

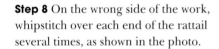

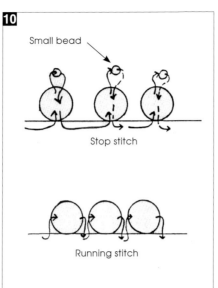

Small bead

Stop stitch

Running stitch

**Step 8** On the wrong side of the work, whipstitch over each end of the rattail several times, as shown in the photo.

**Step 9** If you wish to add beads, work from large to small, sewing on all of one size before sewing on the next size. You can plan the total arrangement first, but remove all but the largest beads when you are ready to sew.

**Step 10** Sew on the beads with the stop stitch or running stitch, following the diagrams above. For a stop stitch, you need a small bead to block the top hole of each large bead.

**Step 11** Next, arrange, pin, and then sew on smaller beads with the stop stitch or running stitch.

**Step 12** Finally, add any other beads you feel are necessary for the composition. I like to put some sort of bead embellishment over the spot where the rattail or other cord element disappears—this way they appear to stop, instead of appearing to go into the fabric. You can see in the photos that I sewed a single bead at each end of the rattail, and then two little strings of seed beads arch over it, too. You can simply sew these beads in place with a single running stitch or stop stitch, but be sure to secure the thread on the wrong side of the work.

⬆ An elegant passementerie-trimmed hat—complete with flowing tassel—can be just the right touch for an otherwise simple evening dress.

# Glossary

**Accordion pleat:** A pleat that looks like a zigzag when viewed in cross section.

**Back of the pleat:** The creased edge of a pleat on the wrong side of the garment or other item. Usually not visible except in an accordion pleat. See illustration on page 134.

**Bias cover:** The bias strip of fabric that wraps the fill for piping.

**Bias strips:** Bias strips should be cut at a 45-degree angle to the selvage of your fabric. The end of each strip must be cut on the straight grain. When joining two strips, lay them flat (right side up) with the ends adjacent, and make sure they lie in a straight line. If they don't, you need to recut one end of one of the strips on the opposite straight grain. Sew bias strips together using a ¼" (6 mm) seam allowance. Press the seam allowances open.

**Bugle beads:** Tubular beads that are measured by the millimeter.

**Chain:** The joined threads produced by the serger when overlocking a seam. The chain secures a serged rolled hem (see page 31), and forms the base for the French seam on page 33.

**Chainette fringe:** Rayon fringe that comes in lengths from 2" to 30" (5 to 76 cm), is available in a wide range of colors, and takes dye easily for color matching. The strands of this fringe are secured with temporary chain stitches to keep them from tangling; remove these chain stitches before you start working with the fringe. See page 147.

**Crystal pleat:** A very tiny accordion pleat. You'll find crystal pleated fabric on bolts in the eveningwear section of a fabric store, or you can have a flat fabric commercially crystal-pleated.

**Curved needles:** Needles that allow you to stitch fabrics to flat hard surfaces and as inside curves, such as hat linings. No sewing studio should be without them. If they are not available in your area, try the local medical supply source—surgical needles are a good substitute. Working with curved needles takes a little practice, so don't give up until you master them. You will be rewarded for your diligence!

**Depth:** The folded area that is concealed under the pleat when the pleat lies closed. The depth is twice the width of the return, and the back of the pleat is in the middle of it (drawing on page 134).

**Fashion fabric:** This is the fabric that will be the outer layer of a finished garment or other project. There are no rules regarding what type of fabric to use or whether the right or wrong side should show in the finished piece (sometimes the wrong side of the fabric is more attractive than the right side). Some people use the terms "front side" and "back side" of the fabric instead of right and wrong sides.

**Favoring:** Favoring is the process of shifting the seamline slightly on one or both pieces to be joined. It allows you to manipulate the seam allowance in a special way or reposition the seam without changing the size of the finished work.

**Fill:** The element used to stuff piping. Many types are available from rattail cord to yarn, in a variety of sizes. The preferred fill used in this book is rattail cord.

**Flange:** Refers to the fabric or twill tape extension that forms the seam allowance on piping; a flat border sewn into a seam that stands out of the seam perpendicular to the surface of the fabric when viewed in cross section; a decorative flat fabric extension on the edge of a project (as on a tailored pillow sham).

**Foundation:** The top edge of chainette fringe, formed by three or five rows of closely spaced, permanent chain stitching that hold the fringe strands together.

**Half-back:** An interfacing piece for the back shoulder area of a jacket or coat, also sometimes referred to as a "back stay." The half-back provides support for the fashion fabric and also a place to attach the shoulder pads (see page 111).

**Home Row:** The first row of beads, usually seed beads, that forms the base of a beaded mesh tassel-knob cover (see page 155).

**Interfacing:** The various materials used to stiffen and support a garment (not to be confused with interlining or underlining). There is usually a separate pattern piece for the interfacing. Interfacing is available in both sew-in and fusible varieties. Unless otherwise stated, sew-in interfacing is the type discussed in this book.

**Interlining or underlining:** These terms refer to fabric that is cut the same size as the fashion fabric and then, with both pieces tailor-basted together, treated as one when sewing for support and weight in the finished piece. These terms are often used interchangeably.

**Knife Pleat:** A single flat pleat or a series of flat pleats that lie one over the other, all facing in the same direction.

**Knob:** The rounded part of a tassel, attached to the hanging cord.

**Leading edge:** The creased edge of a pleat on the right side of a garment or other item (see drawing on page 134).

**Lining:** Lining serves two purposes: first, to finish the inside of the piece, and second, to enhance the appearance of the piece. It is very satisfying to the sewer to know the inside of the piece is as beautiful as the outside, even when no one else sees the lining.

**Machine-Ease:** To ease fabric by machine, shorten the stitch length and sew, holding your index finger on the fabric behind the presser foot so that the fabric bunches up behind the foot. This bunching causes the fabric to ease slightly. Release and reposition your finger frequently so the fabric feeds continuously.

**Mold:** Piece of wood or other material that gives shape to the "knob" of the tassel. The fringe of the tassel hangs from the mold, and the mold can be either covered by the fringe or covered by other materials (see page 158).

**Mushroom pleat:** Also called the "Fortuny" pleat, this pleat is created by knife-pleating the fabric and then box-pleating over the knife pleats. Fabric can be purchased this way or sent out to a commercial pleating establishment.

**Nymo thread:** Spun nylon thread, strong as dental floss, is the reliable "Timex watch" of thread and the best choice for bead mesh (see page 155). Nymo is sized by letter, with size B being a good all-purpose size. For best results, iron the thread before use, because ironing will take out the twist and make the thread less prone to knotting.

**Overlap:** The section of the fabric that covers the zipper on the right side of a project (see page 45).

**Pick Stitch:** A tiny handmade backstitch spaced ¼" (6 mm) apart, and used as topstitching or as the finish that attaches a zipper to the fashion fabric. The pick stitch is quick and easy and screams couture!

**Piping:** A small round trim with a flat extension called a flange that is inserted into a seam. Piping is usually fabric-covered cord, but you can purchase piping made of decorative twisted cord attached to a twill tape flange. (When I met the costume curator at the Los Angeles County Museum of Art, he commented on how much he liked my piping tricks. He said, "Piping is next to godliness." How true! For those of you who avoid using piping because you don't like seeing the initial line of stitching that made the piping once the seam is finished, check out the method on page 45).

**Pleat width:** The portion of the pleat that extends from the leading edge of one pleat to the leading edge of the adjacent pleat (see drawing on page 134).

**Pocket:** Pockets can be very loosely categorized as either patch or set-in pockets. Patch pockets are just what the name implies, a patch that serves as a pocket. A set-in pocket is inserted into a seam or into a slashed opening on the body of a piece. This pocket style almost always has a separate pocket bag. (See chapter 5.)

**Pocket bag:** The part of the pocket that holds the contents. In the pockets here, except for the lined patch pocket, the pocket bag is one or two separate pieces.

**Pocket facing:** The back section of some two-piece pocket bags, cut from the fashion fabric.

**Pocket lining:** The inside layer of a patch pocket, but not to be confused with the pocket bag.

**Prairie points:** Squares of fabric folded into a triangular shape and used as an applied or inserted edge trim.

**Rattail cord:** Satin cord, about ⅛" (3 mm) thick, usually used for decorative work but often used as fill for piping. ("Mouse tail," its cousin, is ¹⁄₁₆" (2 mm) thick.) This cord is made of rayon and comes in a variety of colors.

**Return:** The distance from the leading edge to the back of the pleat (see drawing on page 134).

**Seed Beads:** Small round beads available in a variety of materials and sizes.

**Shields:** Multilayer fabric shapes used to reinforce and give structure to the shoulder area of a tailored garment. They are attached to the body interfacing and smooth out the dip between the collarbone and shoulder joint (see page 116).

**Shoulder Pad:** Also called a shoulder shape, shoulder pads are thicker than shields and contain various types of padding (see page 119). Shoulder pads are inserted between the lining and the interfaced outer layer of the garment to support and give shape to the shoulder and sleeve cap.

**Skirt:** The loose strands of fringe that hang below the knob on a tassel and give it movement.

**Sleeve Cap:** The upper, curved portion of the sleeve that attaches at the top of the armhole. It is usually eased.

**Sleeve Head:** A strip of padding at the top of the sleeve cap. The sleeve head sits between the seam allowance of the cap and the cap itself. It eliminates any puckers caused by easing and helps the cap to mold gracefully by padding it out slightly.

**Thinning:** Trimming the fill out of the bias cover when the end of a length of piping is stitched into a seam. This reduces bulk at the ends of piping so that you can sew across it.

**Underlap:** The hidden section of fabric in a zipper installation that lies behind the overlap (see page 45).

**Understructure:** A generic term applied to all interfacings, interlinings, and support notions used to create the various effects desired. When your work relies heavily on understructure, it is easy to achieve effects that flatter a figure—or even a sofa!

**Waist:** The wrapped section between the knob and the skirt on a tassel (see drawing on page 147).

**Walk the needle:** This phrase is another way to say, "turn the machine wheel by hand in order to sew one stitch at a time."

**Welt:** A flat band of fabric that trims the opening of a set-in pocket. A single welt is attached to the bottom of the opening and conceals the opening itself (see page 89). A double welt is two narrow fabric lips that frame the opening. A welt can also be used for bound buttonholes (see page 109).

**Working above the fabric:** Refers to working only through the holes in the beads to create certain effects. In bead mesh, after the home row is attached to the piece, the needle travels only through the holes in the beads. The needle doesn't stitch into the item inside the mesh.

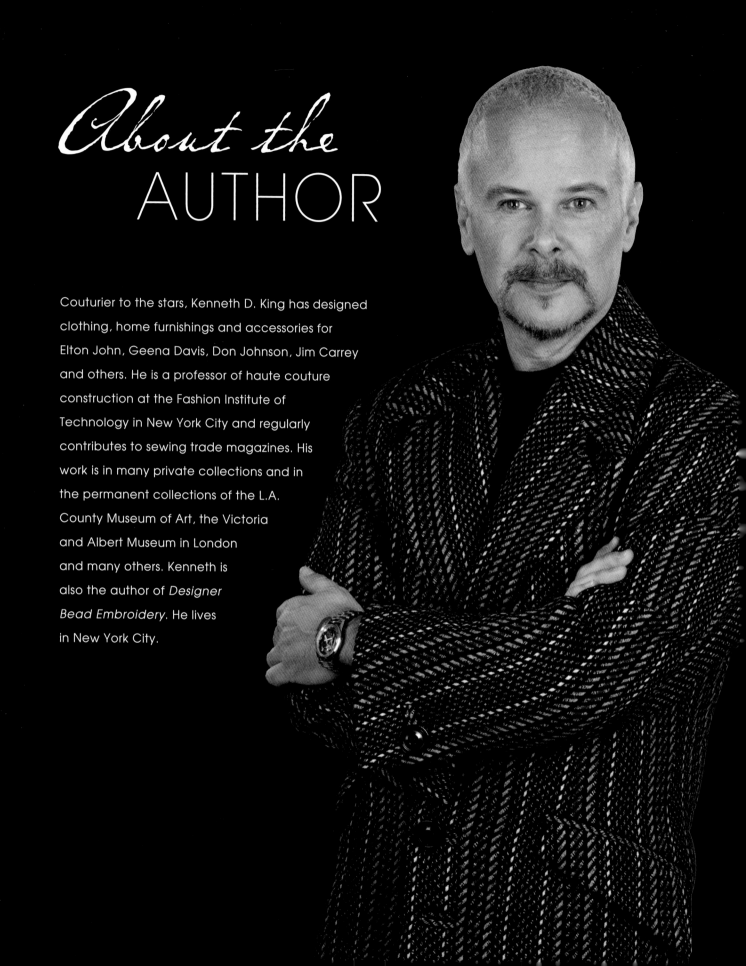

# About the
# AUTHOR

Couturier to the stars, Kenneth D. King has designed
clothing, home furnishings and accessories for
Elton John, Geena Davis, Don Johnson, Jim Carrey
and others. He is a professor of haute couture
construction at the Fashion Institute of
Technology in New York City and regularly
contributes to sewing trade magazines. His
work is in many private collections and in
the permanent collections of the L.A.
County Museum of Art, the Victoria
and Albert Museum in London
and many others. Kenneth is
also the author of *Designer
Bead Embroidery*. He lives
in New York City.

# Index